GEOFF BOND

The Bond Effect

Paleo Harvest

Cookbook

Companion to

Deadly Harvest

Nicole Bond

With

Geoff Bond

First edition © 2013 Nicole Bond
This publication is a creative work fully protected by all applicable rights.

COVER DESIGN: Jeannie Tudor
PRINTER: CPI Antony Rowe Ltd

ISBN-13: 978-0-9927512-0-3

General Websites: www.NaturalEater.com
                           www.TheBondEffect.com
                           www.GeoffBond.com

Paleo Harvest Website: www.Paleo-Harvest.com

e-mail: admin@naturaleater.com

Published by Bond Effect Publications:

7, Maxwelton Close	**111, Leoforos Chlorakas, Unit 9**
London NW7 3NA	**8220 Chlorakas**
England	**Cyprus**

FOREWORD

Nicole Bond's new cookbook encapsulates Geoff Bond's wealth of anthropological research in living the way nature intended (the 'Bond Effect'), also called 'Bond-Paleo'. She creatively transfers these principles into delectable, tasty and healthy new recipes. They hold the key to a simple and effective way to all who are interested in energizing and enlivening their lifestyle.

Eating is a prime ingredient for survival. Eating right is the prime ingredient to a healthy life. And when food preparation becomes simple, enjoyable and tasteful, we have an unbeatable combination. This book contains such ingredients. The shift from eating to dining is simple to make and Nicole shows us how.

Dining is an art. It entails a combination of foods, aromas, sights, environment and attitudes that encourage and promote an elevated sense of the natural treasures we all have available to us. With a graceful sensitivity, Nicole reveals her culinary secrets so all can benefit. Every recipe is designed in accordance with the 'Bond-Paleo' Guidelines. They are tested and refined in the light of the most recent findings making this book a stand-alone guide for a tasteful, healthy dining experience.

The foods, the delights and the results of reading and applying the guidelines in this useful and practical cookbook will provide a quality experience that reaches far beyond eating. In its simplicity lies its power. In its use lie its benefits. In its sharing lies its enjoyment.
Bon appétit.

Dr. James Melton
Visionary & Speaker

PALEO HARVEST COOKBOOK
Companion to Deadly Harvest

CONTENTS

INTRODUCTION

Most of us try to do the right thing by our children and spouses, especially when it comes to feeding them. But we are confused by the conflicting messages. We are inundated with a plethora of diet books and cookery manuals claiming to show us the way to health and happiness. So what is so different about this one? The difference is fundamental. It is none other than feeding ourselves the way Mother Nature intended! That way we avoid stressing our bodies with foods it was never designed to handle. You will draw comfort from the knowledge that, by cooking our way, you are building the foundations for long, healthy lives.

We have designed all these recipes to conform to the principles of The Bond Effect. That is, they are in accordance with the basic guidelines formulated by nutritional anthropologist Geoff Bond. (See later). So when you follow these recipes you know that you are doing the right thing by yourself and your family.

This way of life does not need you to eat in an outlandish way. Your dinner guests will be surprised to find that they have been eating what seem like conventional dishes. Only you will know what subtle, yet vital changes in ingredients – and in cooking – you have made.

The principles behind the recipes of Paleo Harvest

Nature fashioned our bodies to be nourished in a particular kind of way – one that is special to us humans. However, for many generations, we have meddled in a state of ignorance with our food supply. The results have not always been happy ones, leading to 'diseases of civilization', like cancer, heart disease, osteoporosis and diabetes.

Geoff's book 'Deadly Harvest' (see back page) describes how this happened and how we finally know the right way to feed us humans – or as he puts it: "how to put the right gas in the tank"! There are many surprises. We learn that many foodstuffs that we take for granted are secretly undermining our health. But the message is an optimistic one: we do not need to be 'food fascists' – we just need to prioritize what is important and what is not.

In this cookbook we focus on the important issues. Thus you will find that the emphasis is on removing 'bad carbs' and 'bad fats' and privilege the 'good' ones. Consumption of fruits, salads and vegetables should be high. We aim to keep the intake of these up at around 75% of the diet and protein-rich foods down to 25%.

Of course sugar is a recent menace in our food supply and we substitute it with safe alternatives.

We strive to keep sodium (salt) low and potassium high. This happens quite naturally with the high intake of plant food but, in addition, we avoid processed food and keep added salt to a minimum. On the other hand, we obtain sumptuous flavors from the liberal use of aromatic herbs, fresh if possible.

We avoid 'non-human' foods that give our bodies trouble with allergic substances (like 'gluten' and 'lactose'), and 'antinutrients' in plants that are foreign to our bodies. (Antinutrients are naturally occurring poisons that plants make to fight off germs and funguses.)

All this might seem quite unusual, but in practice all we are doing is clearing out foods that have been making us sick for generations and replacing them with ones that work in harmony with our bodies. We invite anyone who is interested in knowing the background to these guidelines to check out Geoff's book, 'Deadly Harvest' (see back page).

Goals

We want you to feel comfortable with this new way of eating. We have devised recipes that follow the guidelines and are simple to prepare. As Geoff says, "we go hunting for our food in the same supermarket, we just hunt smarter!"

Nicole has tested each of the recipes many times to make sure they work well under all kinds of circumstances. We eat them regularly both for our family meals and when we are entertaining. They do not require huge expertise, just basic cooking skills and a willingness to try out new ways of preparing familiar dishes. Be prepared to be adventurous too! Try variations: experiment with different herbs and flavors!

What's in the Cookbook?

We set the scene for you in the segment, called 'Basics'. Here we help you with some of the basic equipment, ingredients and cooking techniques.

Then, with Chapter One, we get into the recipes with simple sauces, dressings and dips. These, from 'Fig Tapenade' to 'Red Onion Relish' or 'Vinaigrette', are always important to give great taste to salads, raw vegetables and other dishes. So often, conventional recipes are loaded with 'bad fats' and 'bad carbs'. But they don't have to be! Here we show you how.

Consumption of large quantities of plant food, preferably raw, is an important feature of the Bond Effect. That is where salads come in – we should all eat at least one good salad a day. Chapter Two focuses on these (e.g. 'Mock Potato Salad', 'Moroccan Carrot Salad' or 'Green Taboulé', as well as a variety of starters, like 'Avocado Salad' or 'Chia Seed Porridge' and 'Paleo Muesli' for your breakfast.

And not forgetting in Chapter Three our special Bond breads like the 'Garlic Flat Bread', our different crackers, basic crusts, and many more.

Chapter Four provides tasty recipes for soups of all kinds, from 'Chicken Goulash Soup' to an 'Oriental Cauliflower Soup'.

In Chapters Five, Six and Seven we come to dishes which can be meals in themselves.

Chapter Five is vegetable-based, like 'Cauliflower Risotto', 'Broccoli Quiche' and many more.

Chapter Six is animal-based (poultry, game and meat), like 'Chili Con Carne' and 'Hunter's Stew'.

Chapter Seven is seafood-based, like 'Avocado and Crab Cake', or 'Prawn Tails in Coconut Sauce'.

Believe it or not, it is quite possible to devise wonderful desserts that conform to the Bond Effect. So, last but not least, with Chapter Eight, we provide a range of remarkable, sugar-free sweetmeats, like cakes and tarts, cookies and muffins, ice creams and even our 'Rich Christmas Cake'. And not to forget our 'Turkish Coconut Delight'.

These dishes are for everyone! Whether or not you decide to live the Bond Effect way, you can be sure that dishes, prepared from this cookbook, will be the healthiest and tastiest that you can offer to your family and guests. Enjoy!

INGREDIENTS, EQUIPMENT & METHODS

For photos of the recipes in this cookbook go to:
www.paleo-harvest.com

SPECIAL PALEO HARVEST INGREDIENTS

It would be wise to have all the basic ingredients available, which are needed to realize the recipes in this book.

Some of the ingredients we use are a little unusual and sometimes they are easiest to buy on the Internet. Or ask your health food store to order them for you. Here we itemize these ingredients and give some explanation as to what they are and why we use them.

Almond Flour (also called Almond 'Powder', Almond 'Meal' or Ground Almond):

We use almond flour in a number of recipes, notably in our bread recipes, to replace wheat flour. As such almond flour is a 'staple' ingredient for eating the Bond Effect way.

Alternatively it is easy to make your own almond flour, simply by grinding raw, blanched and unsalted almonds in a food processor.

You can make a nut-flour from most other kinds of tree nut, particularly hazelnut and cashew.

Adjust the quantities of almond flour in the recipes according to:

- the actual size of the eggs, and

- the texture and density of the almond flour. It makes a difference in volume if it is finely or coarsely ground and if the almond skins are included or not.

Our recipes use exclusively blanched and finely ground almonds.

The consistency should be as described in the recipe. Be patient – you might have to make a couple of trials before you get the right result.

Chia Seeds and Chia Flour:

Chia is the highest known vegetarian source of omega-3 and it also contains powerful antioxidants, vitamins and minerals. Chia is rich in healthy fiber and absorbs water which helps with thickening of dishes. It bulks well, so saving on almond flour and other special 'Bond flours'. The fiber has a gelling property which helps the dough to rise. We find this particularly useful in our bread recipes.

Chia helps to keep your heart healthy, keep your brain sharp, keep your digestive system healthy, enhance your energy, keep you slim and free from joint pain.

Flax Seed & Flax Flour:
Flax contains omega-3, antioxidants and fiber, all essential for a healthy heart, brain and digestive system. We use it in our bread and cracker recipes.

Hemp Seed Flour:
Hemp is another good source of omega-3 essential oil, and it is rich in dietary fiber.

Coconut Flour:
Coconut flour is high in protein and extremely high in healthful dietary fiber. It is relatively low fat (around 15%). It bulks well thus saving on almond flour and other special 'Bond flours' - and it absorbs liquids.

Desiccated/Shredded Coconut:
Desiccated shredded coconut is similar to the flour, although it has a much higher fat content – up to 50%. The chief fat is 'lauric acid' which is an unusual saturated fat. As such it is not harmful like common saturated fats and, moreover, it is not especially bio-available. That is, the body doesn't absorb it well and it passes out, largely undigested, in the stools.

However, it is possible to find defatted desiccated coconut which has a much lower fat content – some 15%. This would be the choice for those wishing to cut down on their fat intake.

The weight per cup of the shredded coconut can vary considerably according to brand. Be prepared to adjust the amounts according to the results you get.

Xanthan Gum:
We use xanthan gum as a binder in baking – in this regard it replaces the role of wheat gluten in helping baked goods to rise. It is quite potent and its efficacy is very sensitive to quantity. You might need to adjust amounts in the light of experience. Xanthan gum is usually made from natural sources.

We use it especially in our bread recipes.

Coconut Milk, Almond (and other tree nut) Milk:

Note: in many countries, including the European Union, the terms 'milk', 'cream' and 'butter' can only be used for dairy products "secreted by milk glands and obtained by milking". However, in the United States, there is no such restriction on these terms.

We use coconut milk and almond milk in a number of recipes. It takes the place of cow (or soy) milk, both of which we need to avoid. Coconut and almond milk are commercially available but do read the labels carefully to avoid those brands that are loaded with added sugars.

Alternatively, you can make your own almond milk or cream. Soak blanched almonds overnight und pulp them, with the liquid, in a food processor. Add water to obtain the consistency desired.

Almond Butter (also Hazelnut Butter, Cashew Butter etc.):

In some recipes we call for nut 'butters'. They can be found in health food stores or online. They are made by grinding the nuts into a fine paste and serve as a spread or substitute for dairy butter.

Stevia:

Stevia is a natural extract of the stevia plant. In its pure form it is an intense sweetener, a pinhead is equivalent to a teaspoon of sugar. Mostly however, it is combined with a filler to bulk it up.

Xylitol:

Xylitol is a 'polyol' (see Diabetic Jam below) and is a natural extract, usually sourced from birch tree bark or other vegetation, including sweet-corn. It is a resistant fiber and it gives the sweetness of table sugar without the sugar rush. It doesn't lose its sweet taste during the baking process.

Diabetic Jam:

We use diabetic jam which, instead of sugar, uses a low glycemic substitute, usually an 'indigestible sugar' known as a 'polyol', like sorbitol or maltitol. Polyols are natural dietary fibers with a sweet taste. See also xylitol above.

A WORD ABOUT:

Bicarbonate of Soda and Baking Powder:

Because our baked goods contain no starch there is nothing for conventional yeast to work on. That is why we use either bicarbonate of soda or baking powder as raising agents. Bicarbonate of soda needs an acid environment to work; baking powder works all by itself – either way allow 10 minutes for the dough to rise.

Salt:

Many of the recipes suggest using salt "to taste". We urge you to keep this added salt to a minimum (the purist will not add any). You will find that, as you retrain your taste-buds, smaller amounts of salt have just the same powerful effect.

Instead of salt learn to use herbs to flavor your food. Lemon juice can give a similar taste sensation to salt. Garlic is good for this too. Mustard is great to give a kick to vinaigrette.

Eggs:

We use eggs a great deal in our recipes. They are always 'large' and always 'omega-3' rich. As such, eggs are a 'staple' ingredient in cooking the Bond Effect way. Contrary to common prejudice, eggs are a natural and healthy component of human nutrition. Fears about their cholesterol content are entirely misplaced: the body handles it in a healthy way. However, always choose eggs that are 'omega 3 rich' (they are more difficult to find – read the labels). They have a much better fatty acid profile: the omega-6 to omega-3 ratio is excellent. In addition, choose eggs from free-range hens (often labeled 'organic' and free of antibiotics.) that have been allowed to lead healthy, sanitary lives,

Raw Eggs:

In the last 20 years our food chain has become so polluted that raw battery hens' eggs are now considered a health hazard. The good news is that organic raw eggs are much safer. This is important in the case of raw eggs, which we use just in a few recipes. Healthy people will have immune systems that cope well with the naturally occurring microorganisms present in eggs. However immune-compromised persons are nowadays obliged to avoid raw eggs.

Oils:

For cooking, we recommend that you use olive oil. It has better heat resistance than omega-3 rich oils like Canola. Always use oils frugally. Think about using an olive oil spray and/or a brush. Learn to sauté with very little oil. See 'Stir-fry and Sautéing' later. Avoid the 'heat resistant' version of Canola oil. That means that the good omega-3 has been stripped out of it.

For cold uses, such as salad dressing, use the omega-3 oils, for example Canola oil. To obtain the full benefit from Canola oil it needs to be cold pressed (you might need to look in a health food store for it). Other good oils are walnut (which must be made from raw walnuts) or flaxseed oil.

Vegetables:

Leave the peel on whenever practicable. Frozen vegetables are often fresher than the so-called fresh vegetables in the supermarket and make a perfectly acceptable alternative. The quality of fresh vegetables is more variable, so the cooking times can vary from those shown in the recipes. The weight of vegetables shown is gross, before cleaning and trimming. The portions of vegetables are larger than you are used to. It is always better to use organic fruit and vegetables if you can. But if you can't, don't let that stop you using regular ones.

Sautéing Onions:

Many recipes call for onions to be gently cooked but not browned. This is the way to do it: spray a non-stick saucepan with olive oil and sauté the onion briefly on medium-high heat. When they start to stick, add some water and cook covered, on low heat. Once in a while, as they dry out, add a little water, to allow the onion to get a very soft consistency. But don't let them brown.

If you have frozen onion, the excess liquid needs to be driven off. Sauté, without oil, until the juices have evaporated. Then add the oil and proceed as mentioned above. Frozen onion cooks much faster.

Sautéing Mushrooms:

Place the sliced mushrooms in a non-stick frying pan without any oil or water. Stir-fry on high heat, stirring constantly until the mushrooms suddenly soften and release their juices. Reduce the heat and add a little olive oil. Optionally, add a little crushed garlic, lemon juice, and chopped parsley.

Salads:

Don't forget that a salad can make an excellent meal in itself. (It is also a good standby when eating out.) Take plenty of mixed salad vegetables together with a portion of the following: salmon, sardine, tuna, mackerel, chicken breast, turkey breast, eggs, etc... It is all right to use canned fish.

Make your own salad dressings (for example vinaigrette page 32), using one of the 'good' omega-3 oils (see 'oils' above).

Tomatoes:

To 'seed' tomatoes, cut them in quarters and carefully squeeze out the pips and juice.

Herbs and Spices:

Use fresh herbs wherever possible. Cut the leaves up with scissors as necessary. For seed spices like pepper, cumin and coriander, the ideal is to use a mill for each and freshly grind them.

Cooked fruit:

Fruit in general is to be avoided at the end of a meal. However, fruit which has been cooked or dried loses its ability to cause digestive upsets and most people can safely consume it at the end of a meal. For this reason, our dessert recipes can include ingredients like raisins or cooked banana.

Vegetable Broth or Juice:

Some of our recipes, notably soups, call for vegetable broth. If you cannot find it, then vegetable juice will do instead. Always go for a low salt version.

You can also make your own vegetable juice by liquidizing your own selection of raw vegetables.

Dark, High Cocoa Mass Chocolate:

Some of the recipes call for chocolate. It must have a minimum of 74% cocoa solids.

Melting of Chocolate:

Some of our recipes call to melt chocolate. We suggest doing it in a microwave oven, but it can also be done in a Bain Marie (porringer).

Cocoa Powder:

Make sure you get pure cocoa powder and not some kind of 'chocolate' mix. Pure cocoa powder is high in antioxidants, especially flavonoids, well known for improving cardiovascular health. Cocoa also contains vital minerals and vitamins such as magnesium, iron, chromium, zinc and vitamin C.

Cheese:

Dairy products are generally to be avoided in ideal human nutrition. Of all the various dairy products, cheese is the least bad: the bad fats pass through the body largely undigested and the lactose has been fermented out. However, the cheese proteins and other compounds still leave a residual nuisance to the body. Some of our recipes use small, condiment quantities of cheese for flavor. However, the purist will leave it out.

Mock Mashed Potato Purée (recipe page 92) as Thickener:

In conformity with the Bond Effect principles, we avoid the use of grain flour, corn starch, potato starch, arrowroot, etc. for thickening. A useful trick is to use instead 'Mock Mashed Potato Purée' (recipe page 92). See how to use it, for example, in the recipe for 'New England Clam Chowder' (recipe page 69).

Ingredients of Animal Origin:

In accordance with the principles of the Bond Effect, a serving of fish, poultry or meat should not exceed 6 ounces.

Game Meats:

We use game meats, such as venison, in some of our recipes. Because they conform to the Bond Effect criteria, they are rather different in nature from farm meats like beef and pork. Game meats are very low fat (less than 4%), and particularly it has no fat within the muscle fibers (as seen as 'marbling' in farm meat). For these very good reasons, venison, and most other conforming game meats, are best tenderized by marinating for 24 hours. We give the instructions in the recipes.

Nutritional Yeast Flakes:

Yeast is popular with the health conscious, where it is often referred to as 'nutritional yeast'. It comes in the form of flakes, or as a yellow powder, and can be found in most health food stores. Because it has a nutty, cheesy, creamy flavor we use it in a few of our recipes for its flavor and thickening properties. It is also a good source of nutrients, particularly B vitamins.

EQUIPMENT
Receptacles:
Because you are now preparing large volumes of plant foods, scale up your ideas of receptacle size. Procure really large salad bowls, mixing bowls, woks and pans.

Ovens:
The recipes in this cookbook are based on baking with conventional ovens.

Fan-assisted (convection) ovens:
Most modern ovens have a fan-assisted option. By blowing the heat around the inside of the oven, it maintains a more even temperature everywhere and the food usually cooks more evenly and more quickly at a lower temperature.

It is good for meat, fish, vegetables and also dishes that are cooked covered. Good for baking bread, cakes and other desserts. It is not so good for dishes that easily splutter.

Microwave ovens:
Contrary to many alarmist reports, cooking with a microwave oven is perfectly legitimate. Depending on the food, it is less aggressive than boiling, frying or roasting, but more aggressive than steaming or sautéing.

COOKING TECHNIQUES
Stir-fry or Sautéing:
Stir-fry is a frequently used 'healthy' cooking method. It may come as a surprise to know that traditional Asian stir-fry doesn't use oil at all. Chinese cooking just uses a couple of teaspoons of water. This is the ideal for us too but it is fine to use an olive oil spray, or a tablespoon (or less) of olive oil. We give quantities in the recipes.

Oil and Water Stir-fry Method:
Try this quick (5 minute) method of cooking vegetables. It starts by steaming and finishes by sautéing. Many vegetables soak up oil and this method greatly reduces the quantity of oil absorbed. Put ¼ inch of water into a large saucepan. Add the vegetables. (If they are frozen they might not need any water at all.) If you like, add a clove of sliced garlic and a bay leaf or a pinch of oregano. Add a teaspoon or two of olive oil according to the volume of vegetables. Cover tightly and cook on high heat. Stir frequently and re-cover. The vegetables cook fast, partly by boiling and partly by steaming. After three or four minutes,

remove the cover and stir-fry continuously with a wooden spoon or spatula until all the liquid has evaporated. Continue until the vegetables are tastily browned on the outside. Do not overcook – this is a quick process – all done in 5 minutes. The vegetables should still be crunchy and be a beautiful golden brown. Always use plenty of herbs.

This is a healthy way of cooking: the vegetables are done quickly and gently in their own steam.

Oil and Water Roasting Method:

This is a sister method for roasting. It is much less aggressive than normal roasting, yet gives a delicious roast-like look and flavor.

Prepare the vegetables for roasting and put them in a roasting pan. Lightly spray or coat them with olive oil and put them in the middle of the preheated oven. Now for the new part: take a baking tray, half fill it with water (about $\frac{1}{4}$ inch), and place it in the bottom of the oven. Cook at the temperature indicated in the recipe for that dish. What happens is this: the water in the tray starts to boil and make steam. The dish is partly steamed and partly roasted. It cooks in about half the normal roasting time and the vegetables come out a lovely golden color.

The high oven temperature boils the water which in turn keeps the cooking temperature at the water's boiling point (212°F, 100°C). In this way the vegetables are cooked more gently. They are also cooked more quickly in the steam. For these two reasons they retain more of their nutrients. Finally the high radiant heat browns the surface of the vegetables.

OVEN TEMPERATURES
Conversion Fahrenheit to Centigrade

Degrees Fahrenheit	Degrees Celsius	Description
250	120	Very slow
265	130	Very slow
285	140	Slow
300	150	Slow
320	160	Moderate
340	170	Moderate
355	180	Moderately hot
375	190	Moderately hot
390	200	Hot
410	210	Hot
430	220	Very hot

VOLUME MEASURE EQUIVALENTS

Cup	Fluid Oz	TBSP	TSP	ml
1 C	8 oz	16 Tbsp	48 tsp	237 ml
3/4 C	6 oz	12 Tbsp	36 tsp	177 ml
2/3 C	5 oz	11 Tbsp	32 tsp	158 ml
1/2 C	4 oz	8 Tbsp	24 tsp	118 ml
1/3 C	3 oz	5 Tbsp	16 tsp	79 ml
1/4 C	2 oz	4 Tbsp	12 tsp	59 ml
1/8 C	1 oz	2 Tbsp	6 tsp	30 ml

CHAPTER 1
Sauces, Dressings & Dips

Artichoke Purée
Yield: 2 servings as a side dish

Can be served as a side dish, accompanying fish for example.
Can also be used as a raw vegetable dip.

14-ounce can artichoke hearts
3 large cloves garlic
1 tablespoon canned capers, drained
3 tablespoons olive oil
2 tablespoons tomato juice, low sodium
1 tablespoon fresh lemon juice
1/2 teaspoon grated lemon peel
2 tablespoons chopped fresh basil
salt to taste
freshly ground black pepper to taste

1. Combine all the ingredients in a food processor and blend coarsely.
2. Can be served hot as a side dish or chilled as a dip.

Sauces, Dressings & Dips
Basil Pesto
Yield: about ½ cup

This is a sauce that is frequently used to flavor soups in Provence and Tuscany. This sauce is also good as a dip for raw vegetables. Experiment with different amounts of the pine nuts and vegetable juice (or broth), to obtain the consistency desired.

The cheese is used in a condiment quantity, but the purist will leave it out.

2 tablespoons raw pine nuts
2 large cloves garlic, roughly chopped
1 cup firmly packed, trimmed fresh basil leaves (about 1 ounce)
2 tablespoons olive oil
4 tablespoons vegetable juice, or broth
1/2 teaspoon grated Parmesan cheese
salt (moderate) to taste

1. Place the nuts in a blender and grind into flour.
2. Add the remaining ingredients and purée until you obtain a very creamy texture.
3. Adjust the seasoning.
4. Keep refrigerated after use.

Sauces, Dressings & Dips
Black Olive Tapenade
Yield: about 2 cups

This is a traditional sauce from Provence. It is served as a spread on a Bond bread (see recipes, pages 49, 50, 52, 54, 59), but can also be served as a raw vegetable dip. If you want to use the tapenade as a sauce, then thin it down, by adding liquid from the olives.

2 cans black pitted olives (6 ounces drained weight each)
5 large cloves garlic, roughly cut
2 tablespoons capers, drained
4 tablespoons olive oil
2 teaspoons red wine vinegar (or balsamic vinegar)
2 teaspoons lemon juice
2 teaspoons thyme, fresh or dried
1/4 teaspoon freshly ground black pepper
6 tablespoons liquid, drained from the olives (more or less as needed)

1. Drain the olives and set aside the liquid (for thinning the sauce, more or less, as needed).
2. Place all the ingredients in your food processor, or blender, and purée until a creamy consistency is obtained. No added salt is necessary, because of the already salty olives.
3. After use, refrigerate any leftovers.

Sauces, Dressings & Dips
Fig Tapenade
Yield: about 2 cups

Serve with crackers (see recipes, page 57, 60) or on a Bond bread (see recipes, pages 49, 50, 52, 54, 59).
Use sparingly, since the fig tapenade is probably rather glycemic.

1 cup dried figs (about 10 pieces)
1/2 cup water
1 cup pitted black olives (about 5 ounces)
1 tablespoon olive oil
1 tablespoon balsamic vinegar
2 teaspoons dried thyme

1. Place figs in a food processor and, using the blade, pulse until finely chopped.
2. Add the water and olives and blend to obtain a smooth paste.
3. Add oil, vinegar and thyme and pulse until smooth.

Sauces, Dressings & Dips
Green Olive Tapenade
Yield: about 2 cups

This is a traditional sauce from Provence (see also the Black Olive Tapenade, page 21).
It is served as a spread on crackers (see recipes, page 57, 60), or on a Bond bread (see recipes, pages 49, 50, 52, 54, 59), but can also be served as a raw vegetable dip. If you want to use the tapenade as a sauce, then thin it down, by adding liquid from the olives.

2 cans pitted green olives (6 ounces drained weight each)
5 large gloves garlic, roughly cut
4 anchovy fillets (canned in olive oil), roughly chopped
2 tablespoons capers, drained
1 tablespoon Brandy
3 tablespoons olive oil
1 teaspoon Herbs of Provence (or Italian seasoning)
6 tablespoons liquid, drained from the olives (more or less as needed)
optional: 2 pinches ground coriander

1. Drain the olives and set aside the liquid (for thinning the sauce, more or less, as needed).
2. Place all the ingredients in your food processor, or blender, and purée until a creamy consistency is obtained. No added salt is necessary, because of the already salty olives and anchovies.
3. After use, refrigerate any leftovers.

Sauces, Dressings & Dips
Guacamole
Yield: 1½-2 cups
(depending on the size of the avocados)

A classic recipe for this excellent dip – and it tastes better than anything you can buy in the shops!

2 ripe avocados
2 tablespoons fresh lime (or lemon) juice
3 tablespoons finely chopped fresh cilantro
1 tablespoon finely chopped green onion
1 large clove garlic, crushed
1 teaspoon ground cumin, or to taste
1/4 teaspoon cayenne pepper, or to taste
1/4 teaspoon salt, or to taste
1/2 cup finely chopped tomatoes (about 3 ounces)

1. Blend all the ingredients (except the tomatoes) in a blender for 20 seconds.
2. Add the tomatoes and pulse for another 5 seconds.
3. Serve chilled.
4. After use, refrigerate any leftovers.

Sauces, Dressings & Dips
Moroccan Tomato Sauce
Yield: about 2 cups
Inspired by Ron Marshall, chef

This versatile and quickly-prepared sauce brings the exotic flavors of the mysterious orient to spice up a variety of dishes. Can also be used instead of Ketchup, or to replace the marinara sauces in the different recipe dishes of this cookbook.

1 tablespoon olive oil
2 medium white onions (about 9 ounces), thinly sliced
3 cloves garlic, crushed
2 cans, 14 ounces each, chopped tomatoes
1 teaspoon ground cumin
1 teaspoon ground coriander
1 teaspoon ground cinnamon
1 1/2 tablespoons xylitol, or to taste
freshly ground black pepper, to taste

1. Heat the oil in a medium-size frying pan and sauté the onion until soft and translucent, but not brown. Mix in the garlic and sauté for 2 minutes.
2. Stir in the chopped tomatoes.
3. Season with the cumin, coriander and cinnamon.
4. Cook uncovered over medium heat, stirring frequently.
5. When most of the liquid has evaporated (after about 25 minutes), reduce the heat. Season with xylitol to taste.
6. Simmer, uncovered, stirring frequently, until the tomatoes start to stick to the pan (the entire cooking time may take up to approximately 40 minutes). Season with pepper to taste.

Sauces, Dressings & Dips
Nacho Cheeze Sauce
Yield: about 1½ cup

This sauce has a cheese-like flavor and is a recipe that will also appeal to vegans.

1/2 cup pine nuts (about 2 ounces)
1/2 cup sesame seeds (about 3 ounces)
1 large clove garlic, crushed
1 red bell pepper (about 7 ounces), seeded and roughly chopped
1 tablespoon fresh lemon juice
1 1/2 tablespoons nutritional yeast flakes
1/4 teaspoon salt, or to taste
freshly ground black pepper, to taste
4 drops Tabasco sauce, or to taste

1. Soak the nuts and sesame seeds overnight (or at least for 3 hours) in water.
2. Rinse nuts and seeds in a sieve (not a colander).
3. Put all the ingredients in your blender, or food processor, and purée until you obtain a smooth consistency.
4. Chill and serve.
5. Refrigerate any leftovers.

Sauces, Dressings & Dips
Onion Curry Sauce
Yield: about 2 cups

This is a delicious and safe to eat sauce, to give added depth and flavor to most vegetable and fish dishes.

olive oil spray
1 medium brown onion (about 5 ounces), thinly sliced
1 teaspoon curry powder, or to taste
1 $\frac{1}{2}$ cups vegetable broth (or vegetable juice), more or less, as needed

1. Spray a non-stick saucepan with the olive oil and sauté the onion briefly on medium-high heat.
2. Mix in the curry to taste.
3. When the onion start to stick to the bottom of the saucepan, add 1/4 cup vegetable broth and cook covered, on low heat, until the onions are soft and translucent.
4. Add more of the remaining vegetable broth, as needed. The sauce is ready to serve.

Sauces, Dressings & Dips

Pearl Onion Relish
Yield: about 3 ⅓ cups

Onions are a wonderful, nourishing supervegetable. This is an interesting way of preparing them with a sweet taste.

This dish is great as a kind of relish to serve with other vegetable dishes or with concentrated foods, such as the olive cake (see page 45). Unlike conventional relishes, this dish can be eaten freely. The small amount of raisins gives taste and some sweetness without increasing blood sugar surges significantly.

olive oil spray
2 packets (10 ounces each) frozen pearl onions
4 tablespoons raisins (about 2 ounces)
1 tablespoon coriander seeds
4 tablespoons white wine
1 tablespoon tomato paste
2 tablespoons balsamic vinegar
2 tablespoons olive oil
1 1/2 tablespoons xylitol
1/2 teaspoon turmeric
freshly ground black pepper, to taste

1. Spray a large frying pan with the olive oil and spread out the frozen onions in a single layer. Sprinkle with the raisins and coriander seeds and start heating the onion on medium heat.
2. In the meantime place all the remaining ingredients in a small mixing bowl, and with a hand whisk, blend until smooth. Pour the mixture over the onions. Bring slowly to a boil.
3. Simmer covered for approximately 40-60 minutes, or until the onions are cooked, but still slightly crunchy.

Sauces, Dressings & Dips
Red Onion Relish
Yield: 3-3½ cups

This makes a highly flavored tangy sweet confection which can be used as any chutney or relish. For example it can accompany any main dish as a condiment complement, such as plain white fish, and many more.

2 tablespoons olive oil
2 pounds red onion, thinly sliced
10 tablespoons red wine
3 tablespoons balsamic vinegar
3 tablespoons red wine vinegar
salt to taste
ground black pepper to taste
6 tablespoons xylitol, or to taste

1. Heat the olive oil in a large sauce pan and sauté the onions on low-medium heat, stirring occasionally, for about 30 minutes, until soft and translucent. Slow cooking is important as this is where the delicious sweet taste will develop.
2. Stir in the wine, the balsamic and red wine vinegar. Salt and pepper to taste. Sweeten with xylitol to taste.
3. Bring to a boil, lower the heat and simmer covered for the first 15 minutes. Then simmer, uncovered, for another approximately 15-25 minutes, or until all the liquid has evaporated.

Sauces, Dressings & Dips
Skordalia Dip
Yield: about 1¼ cups

A classic Greek sauce which can be served as a dip, or served with chicken or fish dishes. As a variant use cold pressed, organic Canola oil instead of olive oil.

3/4 cup blanched almonds (about 4 ounces)
4 large cloves garlic, roughly chopped
1 tablespoon fresh lemon juice
1 tablespoon nutritional yeast flakes
1/2 cup extra virgin olive oil
1/2 cup hot water (more or less, depending on desired consistency)
salt to taste
freshly ground black pepper, to taste

1. Place the almonds in a blender, and grind (on high speed) into flour.
2. Add the garlic, lemon juice and yeast flakes and purée until smooth.
3. Keep the processor running whilst you very slowly pour in the oil.
4. Blend in the water gradually to give the sauce the consistency you prefer.
5. Salt and pepper to taste.
6. Refrigerate prior to serving.

Sauces, Dressings & Dips
Tomato Sauce Provençale
Yield: about 1¼ cups

This highly flavored tomato sauce makes a fine condiment complement to such dishes, as broccoli loaf (page 77) and many more.

1 pound ripe tomatoes*
olive oil spray
1 medium onion (about 4 ounces), finely chopped
3 medium cloves garlic, crushed
1 teaspoon dried Herbs of Provence (or Italian seasoning)
2 bay leaves
salt to taste
freshly ground black pepper, to taste
2 tablespoons chopped fresh parsley

1. In a medium-size bowl pour boiling water over the tomatoes. Set aside for 1 minute. Drain the tomatoes, peel off the skin, cut in quarters, seed and chop them. Set aside.
2. Spray a medium-size, non-stick frying pan with the olive oil and sauté the onion until soft and translucent, but not brown. Add the garlic and sauté for 2 more minutes.
3. Add the chopped tomatoes, the Herbs of Provence (or Italian seasoning), the bay leaves and salt and pepper to taste.
4. Cook uncovered over medium heat. When most of the liquid has evaporated, reduce the heat. Simmer, uncovered, stirring frequently, until the tomatoes start to stick to the pan (this whole cooking process may take 50-60 minutes, when using fresh tomatoes). Mix in the parsley.
5. Can be served hot or cold.

*Alternatively can be replaced by the equivalent in canned chopped tomatoes.

Sauces, Dressings & Dips
Basic Vinaigrette
Yield: about 2 cups

This is a simple, light and salt-free vinaigrette for everyday use in your salads. The use of mustard and lemon juice means that we can dispense with salt. This recipe makes plenty for several uses. It is always easier to knock up a delicious salad when the dressing is ready to hand.

1 cup Canola oil
1/2 cup freshly squeezed lemon juice
2 1/2 tablespoons Dijon mustard
1/2 teaspoon freshly ground black pepper
4 large cloves garlic, crushed
optional: add a variety of chopped fresh herbs, e.g. chives, parsley, basil, cilantro etc.

1. Place all the ingredients, except the fresh herbs (optional), in a medium-size mixing bowl and, with an electric hand-mixer, blend until creamy, scraping down the sides of the bowl as necessary.
2. Mix in the herbs (optional).
3. Keep refrigerated after use.

CHAPTER 2
Salads and Starters

Artist's Salad
Yield: 4 servings

This exotic salad is a favorite recipe of Doros Theodorou, Manager of 5-Star Hotels in Mediterranean resorts.

2 cups roughly chopped fresh rocket (arugula) leaves
2 cups roughly chopped fresh cilantro leaves
3 cups thinly sliced mushrooms (about 6 ounces)
8 tablespoons vinaigrette (see recipe page 32), or to taste
2 cherry tomatoes, cut in half

1. Put the rocket, cilantro and mushrooms in a medium-size salad bowl. Add the vinaigrette and toss well.
2. Serve immediately on 4 individual plates and decorate each serving with one half of the cherry tomatoes.

Salads and Starters
Avocado Salad
Yield: 4 servings

This is a highly nutritious, satisfying salad. Don't hesitate to use it as a main course if you desire.

Vinaigrette:
4 tablespoons Canola oil
2 tablespoons freshly squeezed lemon juice
salt to taste
freshly ground black pepper, to taste
Staples:
2 cups thinly sliced brown or white mushrooms (about 4 ounces)
2 green onions, thinly sliced
3 cups fresh baby spinach leaves (about 2 ounces)
2 avocados, peeled, roughly cut into equal, bite-size chunks
8 cherry tomatoes, cut in half

1. Place the vinaigrette ingredients in a medium-size salad bowl and, with a hand-whisk, blend until creamy.
2. Add the mushrooms, the green onions and the spinach leaves and toss well. Gently mix in the avocado chunks.
3. Decorate with the cherry tomato halves and serve in the salad bowl.

Salads and Starters
Bell Pepper Provençale
Yield: 4 servings

To make the dish more colorful, instead of 4 red bell peppers, you can use 3 red and 1 yellow or orange bell pepper (green bell peppers are less tasty).

4 medium red bell peppers
4 large cloves garlic, crushed
4 tablespoons olive oil
salt (moderate)
freshly ground black pepper, to taste
1 tablespoon chopped fresh basil leaves

1. Wash the bell peppers. Bake in a hot oven at 340°F (170°C) for about 40 minutes, turning them once. Their skin should be wrinkled. Place the bell peppers in a plastic bag and close tightly. Let them cool off in the bag (alternatively: holding the bell pepper in tongs, sear it over a flame until the skin blisters, loosens and chars slightly).
2. Their skin can now easily be removed. Cut in half, to take off the seeds. Remove the stalks and ribs. Cut in 1-inch strips.
3. Lay out the bell peppers in a serving dish.
4. Take a small bowl and, with a fork, mix together garlic, oil, salt and pepper to taste, and half of the basil. Pour this mixture equally over the bell peppers.
5. Keep the dish in the fridge until 15 minutes prior to serving. Best made 2- 3 hours in advance, or even the day before.
6. Prior to serving, sprinkle the remaining basil over the bell peppers.

Salads and Starters
Chia Seed Porridge
Yield: 1 serving

This is a quick fix breakfast starter. It is a terrific and healthful replacement for conventional oatmeal porridge, full of omega-3 fatty acids and natural plant fibers (hence its slightly glutinous nature).

2 tablespoons chia seeds
1/2 cup water*
1 teaspoon vanilla extract
1 tablespoon xylitol, or to taste

1. Place the chia seeds in a small breakfast bowl.
2. Bring the water to a boil and pour over the seeds. Let stand for a few minutes, until it thickens.
3. Stir the mixture thoroughly and season with the vanilla extract and the xylitol to taste.

* The water could be replaced by coconut milk or any tree-nut milk.

Salads and Starters
Deviled Eggs
Yield: 10 Egg Halves

A simple, fully conforming dish that makes a great starter or canapé at a party.

5 large eggs, omega-3
2 tablespoons conforming mayonnaise*
1 tablespoon Dijon mustard
1/4 cup finely chopped parsley
1/4 cup finely chopped celery
1 teaspoon finely chopped shallots
salt to taste
ground black pepper to taste
1/2 teaspoon paprika

1. Hard-boil the eggs. Let them cool.
2. Meanwhile in a medium-size mixing bowl combine the mayonnaise with the mustard. Add parsley, celery and shallots and salt and pepper to taste. Set aside.
3. Take off the egg shells and cut eggs in half.
4. Separate the egg yolks from the whites. Set aside the whites on a serving dish.
5. Mash the yolks with a fork and add to the mayonnaise mixture in the bowl.
6. Fill yolk mixture into egg white halves. Sprinkle the top of each halve with paprika.
7. Refrigerate until serving.

*Conforming mayonnaise: the original – and best – mayonnaise is made only from olive oil, eggs and maybe some lemon juice and mustard. You can substitute Canola (rapeseed) oil for olive oil. If buying ready-made, try to find a product that conforms as closely as possible to these ingredients.

Salads and Starters
Green Taboulé (Tabbouleh)
Yield: 6 servings

Taboulé is normally a Middle Eastern confection based on couscous or bulgur which are both forms of wheat.

Here we replace the wheat flour with white cabbage which, after treatment in the food processor, has a similar grainy texture. This taboulé is humming with a wonderful orchestra of micronutrients. Eat as much as you like!

Vinaigrette:
1 tablespoon Dijon mustard
4 tablespoons canola oil
4 tablespoons lemon juice
salt and pepper to taste

Staples:
6 tablespoons raisins
1 medium onion (about 4 ounces), quartered
1 1/4 pounds white cabbage, cut into large chunks
3 green onions, cut into large pieces
2 green bell peppers (about 10 ounces), seeded and quartered
2 sticks celery (about 2 ounces), cut into pieces
1 small cucumber (about 2 ounces), cut into pieces
5 gloves garlic, cut in half
4 sprigs fresh mint
4 sprigs fresh parsley
1 tomato (3-4 ounces)

1. Place the vinaigrette ingredients in a medium-size mixing bowl and, with an electric hand-mixer, blend until creamy. Salt and pepper to taste.
2. Add the raisins. Set aside.
3. Combine the onion, cabbage, green onion, bell peppers, celery, cucumber, garlic, mint and parsley in a food processor and, using the blade, mix to obtain a coarse consistency.
4. Mix in the vinaigrette and place the dish in your fridge for a few hours (best when prepared the day before).
5. Prior to serving, chop the tomato finely by hand and add to the taboulé mixture.

Salads and Starters
Herby Portabella Mushrooms
Yield: 6 servings

This is an eye-catching starter for a dinner party or cold buffet. Experiment with the coriander and vinegar quantities to suit your taste.

6 Portabella mushrooms, medium-size
olive oil spray
2 tablespoons olive oil
3 tablespoons raspberry vinegar (could be replaced by balsamic vinegar)
3 medium cloves garlic, crushed
1 tablespoon chopped fresh cilantro
3 cherry tomatoes, cut in half
3 cups mixed green leaves (about 3 ounces), e.g. watercress, rocket (arugula), baby spinach, trimmed and washed

1. Wipe the mushrooms carefully with a paper kitchen towel. Trim the end of the stems.
2. Spray the bottom of a medium-size baking dish lightly with olive oil. Place the mushrooms, stalk-side up, in the baking dish.
3. Whisk with a fork, in a small mixing bowl, the olive oil, the vinegar and the garlic. Stir in the chopped cilantro.
4. Divide among the upturned mushrooms. Cap each mushroom stem with a tomato half.
5. Cover with aluminum foil and cook at 320°F (160°C) for approximately 25 minutes (in a microwave it takes only approximately 8-10 minutes at 650 watt power). Check for doneness.
6. Serve the mushrooms on a bed of green leaves.

Salads and Starters
Kelp Noodle Salad
Yield: 6 servings

Kelp noodles are made from an extract of a kind of seaweed, called 'kelp'. They consist chiefly of 'alginate' which is a gum-like dietary fiber. It arrives indigested in the colon where bacteria ferment it into useful chemicals.
Otherwise, kelp noodles have virtually no nourishment and their chief advantage is that they do no harm – unlike conventional pasta.

1 package (12 ounces) kelp noodle
1/2 cup almond butter
1 tablespoon rice wine vinegar
1 tablespoon light soy sauce
1 teaspoon sesame oil
3 tablespoons water
4 cloves garlic, crushed
1 teaspoon grated ginger
freshly ground black pepper, to taste
1 big red bell pepper (about 7 ounces), seeded and chopped
3 celery stalks (about 3 ounces), finely chopped

1. Rinse the kelp noodles thoroughly. Drain and set aside in a large salad bowl. I usually cut the noodles with scissors, in order to obtain shorter noodles.
2. Meanwhile place the almond butter in the food processor. Combine with the vinegar, soy sauce, sesame oil and water and blend all together until you obtain a thick, but creamy sauce.
3. Mix in the garlic and ginger and pepper to taste.
4. Pour the sauce over the noodles and toss to incorporate.
5. Mix in the chopped red bell pepper and celery.

Salads and Starters
Mango Starter
Yield : 2 servings

The mango starter is naturally sweet and slightly glycemic. In these small quantities it is nevertheless acceptable.

1 mango (about 1 pound)
1 tablespoon olive oil
3 tablespoons mango sauce (see recipe below)
1 tablespoon chopped fresh mint leaves (or lemon balm leaves)
freshly ground black pepper, to taste

1. Peel the mango and carve the flesh around the stone into slices. Divide and lay out between 2 plates.
2. Drizzle with olive oil and mango sauce (see recipe below).
3. Sprinkle with the mint leaves and pepper to taste.

Mango Sauce: Yield about 1 1/4 cups
1 mango (about 1 pound)
2 tablespoons raspberry vinegar, or to taste (can be replaced by another fruit vinegar or white wine vinegar)

Peel the mango and carve the flesh around the stone. Purée the flesh with the vinegar (to taste) in a blender until smooth. Pour into a bottle and keep in the fridge.

Salads and Starters
Mock Potato Salad
Yield: 2-3 servings as a main dish
- or 4-6 servings as a starter

This is a yummy dish with an uncanny resemblance in taste and texture to a great potato salad. But this recipe (with no potato) is fully conforming. Eat as much as you like.

It might be necessary to adjust the quantities of dressing (mustard, mayonnaise and oil) to taste.

1 cauliflower head (about 1 1/2 pounds)
1 tablespoon Dijon mustard
3 tablespoons conforming mayonnaise*
2 tablespoons Canola oil
1 medium onion (about 4 ounces), finely chopped
3 celery stalks (about 3 ounces), finely chopped
4 sprigs fresh parsley, finely chopped
freshly ground black pepper to taste
2 eggs, omega-3, hard boiled and finely chopped

1. Divide cauliflower into small florets.
2. Steam for about 10 minutes, until tender but still crunchy. Set aside to cool.
3. Meanwhile, in a large salad bowl, combine the mustard with the mayonnaise and oil.
4. Stir in the chopped onion, celery and parsley. Season with pepper to taste.
5. Add the cauliflower florets and coat well with the ingredients.
6. Carefully fold the chopped eggs into the cauliflower salad.

*Conforming mayonnaise: the original – and best – mayonnaise is made only from olive oil, eggs and maybe some lemon juice and mustard. You can substitute Canola (rapeseed) oil for olive oil. If buying ready-made, try to find a product that conforms as closely as possible to these ingredients.

Salads and Starters
Moroccan Carrot Salad
Yield: 6 servings

The quantities of herbs in this recipe are quite high and they are rich in wondrous micronutrients. Experiment with different quantities of herbs to suit your taste. Fresh parsley and mint are best, but if not, then use dried ones. You need only a quarter of the fresh volume. In contrast, fresh garlic is more potent than ready-to-use preparations.

This salad tastes best when prepared an hour ahead of time and set out at room temperature to develop full flavor.

1 1/2 pounds carrots, peeled
2 cups chopped fresh parsley
1 cup chopped fresh mint
Vinaigrette:
5 tablespoons Canola oil, organic, first pressing
4 tablespoons lemon juice, preferably freshly squeezed
1 teaspoon (or to taste) ground cumin
salt (moderate), to taste
freshly ground black pepper, to taste
1 dash Tabasco Sauce (optional)
6 large cloves garlic, crushed

1. Grate the carrots in a food processor. Set aside.
2. In a large salad bowl make the vinaigrette, by mixing all the ingredients with a hand-whisk.
3. Add the carrots, parsley and mint and toss well.
4. Should be eaten the same day, but keep covered until ready to serve.

Salads and Starters
Multicolored Eggplant Sandwich
Yield: 4 servings

Delight your friends at a dinner party. These multicolored, multilayered 'sandwiches' make a dish that is both spectacular and amazingly tasty, but also easy to make.
Note: this dish, with its cheese, is not for the purist.

2 very large eggplants (about 2 pounds)
1/2 pound Mozzarella cheese
1 pound large tomatoes
olive oil spray
1 cup fresh basil leaves (about 15 leaves per sandwich, garnish included)
4 tablespoons balsamic vinegar

1. Cut the washed, but unpeeled, eggplants into 12 large slices (1/2-inch thick). Set aside.
Cut the Mozzarella cheese into 8 large slices (1/4-inch thick). Set aside.
Cut the washed tomatoes into 8 large slices (1/2-inch thick). Set aside.
2. Spray a baking sheet with the olive oil and lay out the eggplant slices. Preheat the grill in your oven and grill the eggplant for about 7-8 minutes on each side, or until the eggplant is soft.
3. Spray a baking dish with olive oil and lay out 4 single eggplant slices on the bottom of the dish.
Cover each eggplant slice with a Mozzarella slice. Then cover the cheese with a tomato slice. Place basil leaves over the top of the tomato slices.
Now place another eggplant slice on top, followed again by another cheese slice, then tomato slice and basil layer. Cover with one last eggplant slice.
4. Bake in a hot oven at 340°F (170°C) for a few minutes, or until the cheese is melting.
5. Place each 'eggplant sandwich' on a small individual serving plate and pour 1 tablespoon of balsamic vinegar over each. Garnish with a few basil leaves.

Salads and Starters
Olive Cake
Yield: up to 12 servings (slices)

This makes a concentrated, high protein dish that is suitable to serve as an appetizer or as an accompaniment to a main meal. The purist will leave out the cheese.

1 can pitted black olives (6 ounces, drained weight)
5 eggs, omega-3
1 pinch of nutmeg
1 teaspoon baking powder
1 teaspoon mixed spices
1 teaspoon garlic powder
10 drops Tabasco sauce
3 tablespoons olive oil
2 tablespoons white wine
about 1 3/4 cups almond flour (about 6 ounces), more or less for required thickness, depending on size of the eggs
optional: 1/3 cup grated Swiss cheese (about 1 ounce)
salt (moderate) to taste
freshly ground black pepper, to taste
olive oil spray

1. Rinse the olives under water in a colander. Drain and cut olives in half. Set aside.
2. Take a medium-size mixing bowl and, with an electric hand-mixer, beat the eggs, together with the nutmeg, baking powder, mixed spices, garlic powder and Tabasco sauce.
3. Mix in the olive oil, white wine and almond flour. Blend until smooth. The mixture should have the consistency of a very thick soup.
4. Using a fork, stir in the olives and cheese (optional - the purist will leave it out). Season with salt and pepper to taste. Be frugal with the added salt. There is already a lot of salt in the olives (even rinsed) and the cheese.
5. Spray a loaf mold (e.g. 9 inches long, 5 inches wide, 3 inches high) with the olive oil and fill with the mixture.
6. Bake in a hot oven at 340°F (170°C) for about 50-55 minutes. Check the center of the dish for complete doneness.

Salads and Starters
Paleo Muesli
Yield: 6 servings

Traditional muesli, which has oat flakes as a base, is off limits. Here we replace the oats with a nourishing blend of conforming alternatives, notably chia seeds.

You can ring the changes by adding other nuts, like pine nuts, or finely chopped walnuts and pecan nuts.

Muesli:
8 tablespoons chia seeds
2 tablespoons raisins
2 tablespoons sesame seeds
2 tablespoons pumpkin seeds
2 tablespoons chopped almonds
3 tablespoons unsweetened shredded coconut
5 tablespoons xylitol, more or less to taste
1 teaspoon ground cinnamon
Add per portion:
7 tablespoons almond milk, hazelnut milk or coconut milk
optional (per portion):
1 teaspoon vanilla extract
1 tablespoon dried goji berries
2 tablespoons fresh chopped fruit

1. Combine the muesli ingredients and store in a jar.
2. In order to prepare **one serving**, place, say, 4 tablespoons of the muesli ingredients in an individual bowl.
3. Add 7 tablespoons of nut milk to one serving.
4. Wait about 10 minutes for the muesli to thicken.
5. Stir the mixture thoroughly and enhance, if desired, with vanilla extract, goji berries or fresh chopped fruit.

Salads and Starters
Red Bell Peppers with Tomato
Yield: 4 servings

A tasty and interesting way to prepare and present red bell peppers. Your guests will be impressed with the attractive and picturesque appearance.

4 large red bell peppers
olive oil spray
4 medium tomatoes
8 canned anchovy fillets
2 large cloves garlic
freshly ground black pepper, to taste
about 40 fresh basil leaves

1. Cut the bell peppers in half, leave the stalks, but remove ribs and seeds. Spray a roasting tray with oil and lay out the bell pepper halves, cut-side up.
2. Place the tomatoes in a bowl and pour boiling water over them. Leave them for one minute, then drain and slip the skins off.
3. Cut tomatoes in quarters and place two quarters in each pepper half.
4. Snip one anchovy fillet per pepper half into rough pieces. Place with the tomatoes in each pepper half.
5. Peel the garlic cloves, slice them thinly and divide the slices equally between the tomatoes and anchovies. Season with the black pepper to taste (the anchovies alone provide enough salt).
6. Spray each pepper half with olive oil.
7. Place the roasting tray on a high rack in a hot oven at 350°F (175°C). Bake for about 40-45 minutes, or until the bell pepper is soft, but slightly crunchy.
8. Garnish with basil leaves. Serve hot.

Salads and Starters
Tuna-Cabbage Salad
Yield: 4 servings

An extraordinarily tasty combination of great, healthy ingredients – the tuna with its good omega-3 oils, the 'SuperVeg' (cabbage), the tomatoes, the garlic and onion - all full of great micronutrients. Your family will enjoy this so much that you might find that these quantities only stretch for 2 people.

Vinaigrette:
3 tablespoons Canola oil
3 tablespoons fresh lemon juice
3 tablespoons conforming mayonnaise*
3 gloves garlic, crushed
freshly ground black pepper, to taste
salt to taste

Staples:
3 green onions, finely sliced
3 medium tomatoes (about 3/4 pound), chopped
3 medium, pickled cucumbers (about 4 ounces), thinly chopped
2 cans tuna in brine (4 1/2 ounces each), drained
1 can black sliced olives (4 ounces), rinsed and drained
1 packet (about 1 pound) shredded white cabbage (coleslaw)
(may be substituted by a whole cabbage, suitably shredded)
3 tablespoons chopped fresh parsley

1. **Vinaigrette:** place all the ingredients in a medium-size mixing-bowl and, with an electric hand-mixer, blend until smooth, scraping down the sides of the bowl as necessary. Transfer the vinaigrette into a large salad bowl.
2. Mix in the green onions, tomatoes, cucumbers, tuna and olives. Add the cabbage. Salt and pepper to taste and toss well.
3. Prior to serving mix in the parsley.

*Conforming mayonnaise: the original – and best – mayonnaise is made only from olive oil, eggs and maybe some lemon juice and mustard. You can substitute Canola (rapeseed) oil for olive oil. If buying ready-made, try to find a product that conforms as closely as possible to these ingredients.

CHAPTER 3
Breads, Crackers and Crusts

Almond Flour Bread
Yield: about 15-20 slices (depending on thickness)

This is a basic bread. It is very easy to make and has a very satisfactory taste and toasting quality.

The xanthan gum provides the 'stickiness' that gluten would otherwise provide.

Dough:
5 large eggs, omega-3
2 1/4 cup almond flour (about 8 ounces)
2 tablespoons olive oil
2 tablespoons red wine vinegar
1/2 teaspoon salt, or to taste
3/4 teaspoon bicarbonate of soda
1 teaspoon xanthan gum

olive oil spray

1. Combine all the dough ingredients in a food processor and, using the blade, mix them to obtain a smooth consistency.
2. Spray a loaf mold (about 7.5 x 4 x 3 inches) with the olive oil and fill with the mixture.
3. Bake in a hot oven at 340°F (170°C) for about 35 minutes. Check the center for doneness.
4. Allow the bread to cool down before de-molding.

Breads, Crackers and Crusts
Coconut Flour Bread
Yield: about 15-20 slices (depending on thickness)

Coconut flour is different than other flours; a little goes a long way. It is very dry and like a sponge, it soaks up the moisture. This mix makes a light bread – ideal for breakfast. Can be eaten fresh or toasted with a spread of e.g. strawberry jam (see recipe page 203).

Dough:
6 large eggs, omega-3
3/4 cup coconut flour (about 3 ounces)
6 tablespoons olive oil
1/4 teaspoon salt, or to taste
1 teaspoon baking powder

olive oil spray

1. Combine all the dough ingredients in a food processor and, using the blade, mix them to obtain a smooth consistency.
2. Spray a loaf mold (about 7.5 x 4 x 3 inches) with the olive oil and fill with the mixture.
3. Bake in a hot oven at 340°F (170°C) for about 40-45 minutes, or until golden brown. Check the center for doneness.
4. Allow the bread to cool down before de-molding.

Breads, Crackers and Crusts
English Tea Bread
Yield: up to 15 slices (depending on thickness)

This is our conforming version of English tea bread, only we use raisins and goji berries instead of currants. Great with coffee as a continental breakfast, or with afternoon tea.

4 tablespoons raisins
5 tablespoons dried goji berries
1/2 cup chopped walnuts (about 2 ounces)
4-6 tablespoons cold, strong-brewed breakfast tea
5 eggs, omega-3
1/2 cup coconut flour (about 2 ounces)
1/2 cup flax seed flour (about 2 ounces)
1 teaspoon baking powder
1/2 teaspoon xanthan gum
3 tablespoons olive oil
1 tablespoon vanilla extract
3 1/2 tablespoons xylitol, or to taste
olive oil spray

1. Combine the raisins, goji berries and walnuts in a medium-size bowl. Combine with 4 tablespoons of cold tea. Set aside to soak.
2. Meanwhile beat the eggs, the coconut flour and flax seed flour with an electric hand-mixer in a medium-size mixing bowl. Blend in the baking powder, xanthan gum, olive oil, vanilla extract and sweeten with xylitol to taste.
3. If required for final dough consistency, add the remaining tablespoons of cold tea
4. Spray a loaf mold (about 7.5 x 4 x 3 inches) with the olive oil and fill with the mixture.
5. Bake in a hot oven at 340°F (170°C) for about 40 minutes. Check the center for doneness.
6. This bread achieves its best when you let it cool down and leave for a couple of hours.

Breads, Crackers and Crusts
Garlic Flat Bread
Yield: about 25 slices (depending on thickness)

This is the right way to do garlic bread - by mixing the garlic into the dough itself (and not simply spreading garlic on the bread slice after baking).

I roast the garlic first - this gives it a mellower flavor. Then I take the Three Flour Bread ingredients (page 59) and mix in the garlic.

2 whole heads of garlic
1 teaspoon olive oil
Dough:
5 eggs, omega-3
1 1/2 cup almond flour (about 6 ounces)
1/4 cup Chia seed flour (about 1 ounce) - or flax seed flour
3 tablespoons chia seeds
2 tablespoons coconut flour
3 tablespoons olive oil
2 tablespoon red wine vinegar
1/4 teaspoon salt, or to taste
3/4 teaspoon bicarbonate of soda
1/2 teaspoon xanthan gum

olive oil spray
optional: 3 teaspoons dried thyme
3 teaspoons dried oregano

1. Using a sharp knife, slice off the very top of each head of garlic. Wrap them separately in foil and drizzle the olive oil over each head of garlic.
2. Bake in a hot oven at 340°F (170°C) for about 35 minutes, or until the garlic is very tender. Set aside to cool.
3. Now pop out the roasted garlic cloves and mash them up with a fork. It's all right if some whole garlic bits remain in the mash.
4. Meanwhile combine all the dough ingredients in a food processor and, using the blade, mix them to obtain a smooth consistency. Mix in the mashed garlic, using a fork and make sure to distribute the garlic evenly into the dough. Optional: incorporate 2 teaspoons of each of the dried herbs.

Breads, Crackers and Crusts

5. Line a baking tray with non-stick baking paper. Spread out the dough mixture with a spatula, to form a rectangular size of about 6x9 inches and about 1 inch thickness.

Optional: spray a little olive oil over the top and sprinkle with the remaining dried herbs.

6. Bake in a hot oven at 340°F (170°C) for about 35 minutes. Check the center for doneness.

Breads, Crackers and Crusts
Olive Bread
Yield: about 25 slices (depending on thickness)

This Greek-style olive bread has a great crust and the interior crumb has a nice chewy texture. It resembles a classic rough-ground whole-wheat bread with, of course, the olives.

1 can pitted black olives (6 ounces, drained weight)
Dough:
5 eggs, omega-3
1 1/2 cup almond flour (about 6 ounces)
1/4 cup flax seed flour (about 1 ounce)
3 tablespoons chia seeds
2 tablespoons coconut flour
3 tablespoons olive oil
2 tablespoons red wine vinegar
1/4 teaspoon salt, or to taste
3/4 teaspoon bicarbonate of soda
1/2 teaspoon xanthan gum

olive oil spray

1. Rinse the olives under water in a colander. Drain and cut olives in half. Set aside.
2. Combine all the dough ingredients in a food processor and, using the blade, mix them to obtain a smooth consistency.
3. Using a fork, incorporate the olives.
4. Spray a loaf mold (about 7.5 x 4 x 3 inches) with the olive oil and fill with the mixture.
5. Bake in a hot oven at 340°F (170°C) for about 50 minutes. Check the center for doneness.

Breads, Crackers and Crusts
Pizza Crust
Yield: one 10-inch crust

Conventional pizza is notoriously heart damaging, raising cholesterol levels and sending blood sugar levels sky-high.

Enter our heart-friendly pizza crust! Low glycemic, diabetic friendly - it uses only conforming ingredients.

1 egg, omega-3
1 tablespoon olive oil
1/4 teaspoon baking powder
1/4 teaspoon xanthan gum
1/4 teaspoon salt
1 1/2 cups almond flour (about 6 ounces)
optional: 1/3 teaspoon garlic powder

1. Beat the egg in a medium-size mixing bowl with an electric hand-mixer, together with the olive oil, baking powder, xanthan gum and salt. Add the almond flour and (optional) the garlic powder and blend until thoroughly combined to a pastry of thick consistency. Use your hands to knead the dough and form into a ball.

2. Place the dough between 2 sheets of non-stick baking paper and roll out into a 10-inch diameter circle.

3. Remove the top baking paper. Transfer the bottom piece of baking paper with the dough onto a baking tray (or alternatively you may want to flip over the rolled-out dough into an oiled, round 10-inch diameter baking dish). Using your hands, press to leave a low rim around the edges. Prick the bottom of the dough with a fork.

4. Bake in a hot oven at 320°F (160°C) for about 10 minutes, to set the dough.

5. Remove from oven and fill with your favorite toppings while still warm.

Breads, Crackers and Crusts
Savory Paleo Crust
Yield: one 9-inch or 10-inch crust

This fully-conforming crust can be substituted for conventional dough in your favorite savory recipes. See also my recipe 'Spinach Quiche' (see page 102).

1 1/2 cups almond flour (about 6 ounces)
4 tablespoons olive oil
1/2 teaspoon baking powder
1 teaspoon xanthan gum
1/2 teaspoon garlic powder
1/4 teaspoon salt
2 tablespoons water, or more if needed
optional: 1 tablespoon chia seeds (or sesame seeds)
olive oil spray

1. Take a medium-size mixing bowl and, with an electric hand-mixer, beat the almond flour with the olive oil, baking powder, xanthan gum, garlic powder and salt. Add the water as needed for required consistency. Mix thoroughly until combined to a pastry of thick consistency.
2. Optional: mix the chia seeds into the dough. Use your hands to knead the dough and form into a ball.
3. Spray a round 9-inch or 10-inch diameter baking dish with the olive oil. Using your hands, press the dough into the dish, by leaving a low rim around the edges. Prick the bottom of the dough with a fork.
4. Bake in a hot oven at 340°F (170°C) for about 10 minutes, to set the dough.
5. Allow to cool completely before filling.

Filling Suggestion:
Beat 3 eggs with 2 cups of 'Red Onion Relish' (see recipe page 29).
Decorate with fillets of anchovies to taste.
Bake in a hot oven at 340°F (170°C) for about 30 minutes, or until the eggs are cooked.

Breads, Crackers and Crusts
Sesame and Walnut Crackers
Yield: about 30 crackers (2-inch diameter)

These crackers are a wonderful support for a huge variety of canapé items.

Other serving suggestions: spread with fig or olive tapenade (see recipes pages 21, 22, 23).

1/2 cup walnuts (about 2 ounces)
1 1/2 cup almond flour (about 6 ounces)
1/2 teaspoon salt
1 egg, omega-3
1 tablespoon olive oil
2 tablespoons sesame seeds

1. Chop the walnuts finely in a food processor, using the blade. Set aside.
2. Combine almond flour, salt, the egg and the olive oil in the food processor and, using the blade, mix to obtain a dough.
3. Transfer the dough to a medium-size mixing bowl. Add the chopped walnuts and the sesame seeds and, using your hands, knead all together. Form into a ball.
4. Lay out the ball of dough onto a non-stick baking paper and flatten with your hands. Place another sheet of non-stick baking paper over the dough.
5. Roll out the dough, between these two pieces of baking paper, until it is cracker-thin.
6. Remove the top baking paper and cut the dough, with the help of a 2-inch diameter cookie cutter, into about 30 round crackers.
7. Bake in a hot oven at 340°F (170°C) for about 12 minutes, or until golden brown.
8. Store in your fridge in a sealed container.

Breads, Crackers and Crusts
Sweet Paleo Crust
Yield: one 9-inch or 10-inch crust

This fully-conforming crust can be substituted for conventional dough in your favorite dessert recipes (see e.g. Apricot Tart, page 154 and Lemon Meringue Tart, page 181).

1 1/2 cups almond flour (about 6 ounces)
4 tablespoons olive oil
1/4 teaspoon baking powder
1 teaspoon xanthan gum
1 tablespoon xylitol
2 tablespoons water, or more if needed
olive oil spray

1. Take a medium-size mixing bowl and, with an electric hand-mixer, beat the almond flour with the olive oil, baking powder, xanthan gum and xylitol. Add the water as needed for required consistency. Mix thoroughly until combined to a pastry of thick consistency. Use your hands to knead the dough and form into a ball.
2. Spray a round 9-inch or 10-inch diameter baking dish with the olive oil. Using your hands, press the dough into the dish, by leaving a low rim around the edges. Prick the bottom of the dough with a fork.
3. Bake in a hot oven at 340°F (170°C) for about 10 minutes, to set the dough.
4. Allow to cool completely before filling.

Breads, Crackers and Crusts
Three Flour Bread
Yield: about 25-30 slices (depending on thickness)

This is my favorite bread recipe. Do not hesitate to experiment a little with the ingredients.

The xanthan gum provides the 'stickiness' that gluten would otherwise provide.

Dough:
6 large eggs, omega-3
2 cups almond flour (about 7 ounces)
5 tablespoons flax seed flour
3 tablespoons coconut flour
5 tablespoons chia seeds
4 tablespoons olive oil
3 tablespoon red wine vinegar
1/4 teaspoon salt, or to taste
3/4 teaspoon bicarbonate of soda
3/4 teaspoon xanthan gum

olive oil spray

1. Combine all the dough ingredients in a food processor and, using the blade, mix them to obtain a smooth consistency.
2. Spray a loaf mold (about 7.5 x 4 x 3 inches) with the olive oil and fill with the mixture.
3. Bake in a hot oven at 340°F (170°C) for about 45-50 minutes. Check the center for doneness.
(If you use fan heat, then cook at 320°F - 160°C, for around 40 minutes.)
4. Allow the bread to cool down before de-molding.

Breads, Crackers and Crusts
Three Flour Crackers
Yield: 25-30 crackers (2-inch diameter)

These crackers (or wafers) make a tasty and practical support for a huge variety of canapé items. Try them with cod liver pâté, nut butter or our Nutella Bond (see recipe page 185).
The dough could also make a wonderful pizza base (roll into a 10-inch circle, 1/8-inch thick).

1 1/2 cup almond flour (about 6 ounces)
1/4 cup Chia seed flour (about 1 ounce) - or flax seed flour
2 tablespoons coconut flour
1/4 teaspoon salt
1 large egg, omega-3
2 tablespoons water
1 tablespoon sesame seeds (or chia seeds)

1. Combine almond flour, Chia seed flour (or flax seed flour), coconut flour and salt in a medium-size mixing bowl.
2. Using a hand-whisk, beat the egg with the water in a small mixing bowl and add to the flour ingredients. Mix in the sesame seeds (or chia seeds).
3. Use your hands to knead the dough to obtain a smooth consistency and form into a ball. Divide into 2 pieces.
4. Place 1 piece of dough between 2 sheets of non-stick baking paper.
5. Roll out the dough between these two pieces of baking paper until it is wafer thin.
6. Remove the top baking paper and cut into wafers (you may use a say, 2-inch diameter cookie cutter). Transfer the bottom piece of baking paper on a baking sheet.
7. Bake in a hot oven at 320°F (160°C) for 18-20 minutes, or until golden brown.
8. Repeat the process with the remaining piece of dough and any leftovers from it.
9. Store in the fridge in a sealed container.

CHAPTER 4
Soups

Chicken Goulash Soup
Yield: up to 6 servings

This is a delicious recipe for that traditional Hungarian, spicy and slightly piquant soup, Goulash. Here we replace the traditional 'bad' red meat (beef, pork, veal or lamb) with chicken.

olive oil spray
2 medium white onions (about 9 ounces), finely chopped
1 skinless chicken breast (about 1/2 pound), cut into 1/2-inch cubes
2 cups tomato sauce, e.g. Napolitano style
2 cups chicken broth or chicken stock
1 large red bell pepper (about 1/2 pound), seeded and chopped
1 teaspoon paprika powder, or more to taste
salt to taste
freshly ground black pepper, to taste

1. Spray a large saucepan with the olive oil and sauté the onion until soft and translucent, but not brown.
2. Add the chicken cubes and sauté for a few minutes from both sides, until golden brown.
3. Add the tomato sauce, the broth and the bell pepper.
4. Season with paprika powder, salt and pepper to taste.
5. Simmer over medium heat for about half an hour, or until the chicken is tender.
6. Best served reheated the next day.

Soups
Chilled Tunisian Tomato Soup
Yield: up to 8 servings

A refreshing and tasty soup whose subtle flavors hint at the mysteries of Arabia.

4 pounds ripe Roma tomatoes, peeled and roughly cut
4 large cloves garlic, roughly cut
2 tablespoons fresh mint leaves
2 tablespoons fresh lime juice
1/2 teaspoon salt (or to taste)
freshly ground black pepper, to taste
Garnish:
8 fresh mint leaves
1 lime, thinly sliced

1. Combine the tomatoes, garlic, mint and lime juice in a food processor (or blender) and purée until smooth.
2. Season with salt and pepper to taste.
3. Serve chilled in individual soup bowls.
4. Garnish with the remaining mint leaves and hook a thin slice of lime on the rim of each bowl.

Soups
Chunky Winter Veggie Soup
Yield: up to 8 servings

This is a quick fix recipe and can be combined differently with other vegetables.
See also different serving suggestions below.

2 large onions (about 12 ounces), roughly sliced
3 celery stalks (about 3 ounces), sliced
2 medium tomatoes (about 12-14 ounces), roughly chopped
1 yellow bell pepper (about 6 ounces), sliced
1/2 white cabbage (about 1 pound), chopped
2 pounds mixed broccoli and cauliflower florets, fresh or frozen
4 cups vegetable broth (about 1 liter), more or less if needed
1 tablespoon thyme, fresh or dried
2-3 tablespoons mild curry paste, to taste
freshly ground black pepper, to taste
3 tablespoons chopped fresh parsley

1. Combine all the vegetables in a large sauce pan.
2. Add the vegetable broth and bring to a boil.
3. Reduce heat, add the thyme and mix in the curry paste to taste.
4. Simmer for about 15-20 minutes, or until the veggies are done, but still crunchy.
5. Prior to serving, season with pepper and stir in the parsley.

Serving suggestions:
In order to make a thicker soup, take half of the volume of the soup and blend it in a food processor. Return to the sauce pan with the remaining vegetables.
Combine with chicken breast, cut into cubes and simmer in the soup broth for the last 10 minutes of cooking time.
Or combine with white fish, cut into cubes and simmer in the soup broth for the last 5 minutes of cooking time.
Or combine with canned, fresh or frozen shrimps, and simmer in the soup broth for the last 5 minutes of cooking time.

Soups
Exotic Broccoli Soup
Yield: 6 servings

A delicious and healthful soup which blends the flavors of Thai cuisine with those of the Middle East.

4 pounds broccoli florets, fresh or frozen
2 white medium onions (about 10 ounces), cut in quarters
4 cups vegetable broth (about 1 liter)
1/4 cup (about 2 ounces) ready-made sesame paste, also called 'tahini'
1 cup light coconut milk
1 tablespoon mild curry paste, or to taste
2 teaspoons ground cinnamon, or to taste
freshly ground black pepper, to taste

1. Steam the broccoli florets and onion quarters for about 15 minutes, or until tender.
2. Place in a food-processor (or blender), add the vegetable broth and mix until smooth.
3. Mix in the sesame paste, coconut milk and season with curry, cinnamon and pepper to taste.
4. Prior to serving, heat in a saucepan.

Soups
Fennel Gazpacho
Yield: 6 servings

The interesting flavor of fennel brings a new excitement to this classic, thick, cold soup.

1 large fennel (about 10 ounces)
2-3 firm Roma tomatoes (about 8 ounces)
2 1/2 pounds ripe tomatoes
1 tablespoon olive oil
1 medium onion (about 5 ounces), chopped
3 cloves garlic, crushed
1 teaspoon ground coriander
1/2 teaspoon freshly ground black pepper
1 teaspoon dried oregano
1 tablespoon balsamic vinegar
2 tablespoons tomato paste
salt to taste
2 cups vegetable broth, or vegetable juice
1-2 tablespoons lime (or lemon) juice, to taste

1. Trim the green fronds from the fennel bulb and save for garnish. Cut fennel bulb into quarters. Chop 3 quarters roughly and set aside. Cut the remaining quarter into very small dices and set aside separately.
2. Cut the Roma tomatoes in halves, seed and cut in very small dices. Set aside separately.
3. Put the tomatoes in a large bowl and pour boiling water over them. Set aside for 1 minute. Drain the tomatoes, peel off the skin, cut in quarters, seed and chop them roughly. Set aside.
4. Heat the oil in a large saucepan and sauté the onion, until soft and translucent, but not brown.
5. Add the garlic, coriander, pepper and oregano and sauté for about 2 minutes, until the spices give off their full aroma. Mix in the vinegar.
6. Stir in the tomato paste and add the roughly chopped tomatoes. Salt to taste.
7. Add the roughly chopped fennel quarters and the vegetable broth. Bring slowly to a boil. Simmer, uncovered, for about 20 minutes, or until the vegetables are cooked. Allow to cool.

Soups

8. Blend the mixture in a food-processor (or blender) until smooth. Add the lime juice (to taste).

9. Stir the fennel dices and Roma tomato dices into the soup.

10. Chill for several hours in the fridge. Prior to serving, chop the fennel fronds and sprinkle them as garnish over the dish.

Soups
Hot and Sour Chicken Soup
Yield: up to 8 servings

This makes a fully conforming soup, emulating the Asian classic. It is full of flavors conjuring up the images of the Orient.

Broth:
8 cups (about 2 liters) water
4-6 fresh coriander roots
1 small onion (about 2 ounces), cut in half
3 garlic cloves, cut in half
2 inches peeled fresh ginger, cut in half
3 bay leaves
1 teaspoon dried lemon grass (or 2 inches fresh stalk, chopped)
1/2 teaspoon black pepper corns
2 skinless chicken breasts (about 1 pound)

1 cup (about 1 ounce) dried Shitake mushrooms
olive oil spray
2 medium onions (7-8 ounces), chopped
1 can (about 5 ounces) bamboo shoots, drained und cut in pieces
1 1/2 cups (about 6 ounces) canned soy bean sprouts, drained
2 medium tomatoes (about 12 ounces), seeded and chopped
1 big red bell pepper (about 7 ounces), seeded and chopped
3 teaspoons Sambal Oelek (for a mild hot taste) – can be replaced by any other chili sauce
6 tablespoons rice vinegar, or to taste
3 eggs, omega-3
2 green onions, chopped

1. To prepare the broth, take a large saucepan and pour in the water. Then add all the broth ingredients, except the chicken breasts. Bring the broth to a boil and then add the chicken breasts.
2. Reduce heat and simmer for at least 30 minutes to bring out the chicken flavor in the broth.
3. Meanwhile soak the mushrooms in boiling water for 5 minutes. Drain, chop the bigger ones and set aside.
4. Take out the chicken breasts, cut in bite-size pieces, cover and set aside.

Soups

5. With a straining spoon remove the other broth ingredients. Reserve the onion, garlic and ginger, chop and return to the broth.

6. Spray a frying pan with the olive oil and sauté the onion until translucent, but not brown. Mix in the bamboo shoots and sauté for a few minutes.

7. Add the bean sprouts, tomatoes and bell pepper to the frying pan and sauté all together for 10 minutes, or until the vegetables are done.

8. Add the mushrooms to the vegetables. Season with Sambal Oelek and rice vinegar to taste. Simmer all together for another 2 minutes.

9. Add the vegetable mixture to the broth in the saucepan, together with the chicken pieces.

10. Beat the eggs with a fork and drizzle the liquid very slowly into the soup, stirring all the while, which creates the filament effect.

11. Ladle the soup into individual bowls and garnish with the chopped green onions.

Soups
New England Clam Chowder
Yield: up to 8 servings

This recipe was featured by the food editor Sue Rappaport, in the Southern California newspaper, the Desert Sun, in December 2002.

Originally chowder was a hearty seafood soup, prepared in a 'chaudière' (cauldron), by Breton fishermen in Newfoundland. The New England variant is made with clams, and it usually includes potatoes, flour and cream. The clams are a fine, conforming seafood, low in fat and cholesterol. We dispense with the three bad ingredients: potatoes, flour and cream and thicken with 'Mock Mashed Potato Purée' (see page 92) As an option, replace the almond milk by chopped tomatoes. This version is known as 'Manhattan-style' chowder.

28-ounce can baby clams
1 tablespoon olive oil
5 green onions, thinly sliced
3 cloves garlic, crushed
2 pounds 'Mock Mashed Potato Purée' (see recipe page 92)
2 1/2 cups almond milk (more or less – as needed for thickness)
celery salt, to taste
freshly ground black pepper, to taste

1. Drain the clams in a colander, but collect the liquid, which will amount to approximately 2 cups (1/2 liter). Set aside.
2. Heat the olive oil in a large saucepan and sauté the green onion and garlic briefly.
3. Add the liquid from the clams. Mix in the 'Mock Mashed Potato Purée' and blend until smooth. Add the almond milk to obtain the right consistency (more or less depending on desired thickness).
4. Bring slowly to a boil. Add the clams and heat slowly through, without further cooking. Season with the celery salt and pepper to taste (be frugal with the celery salt, because of the already very salty clam liquid).

Soups
Oriental Cauliflower Soup
Yield: up to 6 servings

The basic idea for this recipe came from Bond Precept practitioner, Jeanne Bouvet, who is concurrently publishing her own recipe book in French, 'La Méthode Bond'.

olive oil spray
1 white medium onion (about 5 ounces), chopped
1 clove garlic, sliced
4 celery stalks (about 4 ounces), sliced
3/4 pound cauliflower florets, fresh or frozen
3 cups water
1 1/2 cups light coconut milk
2 teaspoons mild curry powder, or more to taste
1 teaspoon ground coriander, or to taste
salt, to taste
ground black pepper, to taste
2 tablespoons chopped fresh cilantro

1. Spray a non-stick frying pan with the olive oil and sauté the onion, until soft and translucent, but not brown.
2. Stir in the sliced garlic and celery and sauté for 3 minutes on medium-high heat.
3. Mix in the cauliflower florets. Add the water and coconut milk. Season with the curry, coriander, salt and pepper to taste.
4. Cover and bring to a boil. Then reduce heat and simmer gently for about up to 35 minutes, or until the cauliflower is done.
5. Purée the cauliflower mixture in your blender (or food processor), until smooth.
6. Prior to serving, sprinkle with the chopped cilantro.

Soups
Red Soup
Yield: 4 servings

A delicious soup that can be eaten cold or hot. It has a massive content of flavonoids in the tomatoes and bell peppers.

4 medium red bell peppers (about 1 1/2 pounds)
28-ounce can chopped tomatoes,
(or 2 pounds fresh ripe Roma tomatoes, peeled, seeded and roughly cut)
3 tablespoons nutritional yeast flakes
2 teaspoons lime juice, or lemon juice
1/4 teaspoon salt
freshly ground black pepper, to taste
10 drops Tabasco sauce, or to taste
3 tablespoons chopped fresh basil
Garnish:
12 fresh basil leaves

1. Wash the bell peppers. Bake in a hot oven at 340°F (170°C) for about 40 minutes, turning them once. Their skin should be wrinkled. Place the bell peppers in a plastic bag and close tightly. Let them cool off in the bag.
2. Their skin can now easily be removed. Cut in half, remove the seeds, stalks and ribs and cut roughly.
3. Combine the bell peppers, the tomatoes and all the other ingredients in a food-processor (or blender), and using the blade, purée to obtain a smooth consistency.
4. Adjust the seasoning to taste.
5. Serve, hot or cold, in individual bowls and decorate with the basil leaves.

Soups
Zucchini Soup
Yield: 4 servings

This is an attractive and interesting way to prepare that normally bland vegetable, zucchini.

about 2 pounds zucchini, unpeeled and roughly chopped
1 medium white onion (about 5 ounces), quartered
3 cloves garlic, roughly cut
4 cups vegetable broth (about 1 liter), or vegetable juice
salt to taste
freshly ground black pepper, to taste
2 tablespoons chopped fresh parsley
1 egg yolk

1. In a large saucepan combine the zucchini, onion and garlic in the vegetable broth. Bring to a boil and cook for about 15-20 minutes.
2. Salt and pepper to taste. Mix in 1 tablespoon of parsley.
3. Place the mixture in a food-processor or blender and mix until smooth.
4. Pour the mixture back in the saucepan and bring slowly to a boil again. Simmer for another 2 minutes. Remove from the heat.
5. Prior to serving, combine the egg yolk in a small bowl with 2 tablespoons of warm soup (not boiling), before stirring it back into the soup.
6. Serve in individual soup bowls and sprinkle the remaining parsley over the top.

CHAPTER 5
Vegetable Dishes

Andalusian Vegetable Medley
Yield: 4 servings

This preparation makes a great main dish or can be used as a tasty (cold) party snack.

1 tablespoon olive oil
2 medium red onions (about 10 ounces), roughly sliced
2 red bell peppers (about 1 pound), seeded and cut into 1-inch strips
6 cloves elephant garlic, sliced
2 tablespoons balsamic vinegar
2 tablespoons light soy sauce
freshly ground black pepper, to taste
1 big eggplant (about 1 pound), unpeeled, cut into 1/2-inch slices
salt (moderate)

1. Heat the oil in a big frying pan (or wok) and sauté the onion, bell pepper and elephant garlic for about 10 minutes, stirring frequently.
2. Stir in the vinegar, 1 tablespoon of the soy sauce and sprinkle with pepper to taste. Sauté all together for 2 minutes.
3. Add the eggplant slices and sprinkle with the remaining tablespoon of soy sauce. Add pepper to taste. Press the eggplant slices gently into the mixture. Cover and bring to a boil. Then reduce the heat and simmer gently for about 30-40 minutes, or until the eggplant is done.
4. If there is too much liquid, cook uncovered for a few minutes, until the liquid has evaporated – or if the vegetables are already very soft, simply remove the excess liquid with a spoon. Salt to taste, but be very frugal, because of the already salty soy sauce.
5. Can be served hot or cold.

Vegetable Dishes
Bohemian Red Cabbage
(Rotkraut)
Yield: 4 servings

This is a delicious dish that has its origins in Central Europe. Traditionally this dish is cooked for up to 1 1/2 hours, until the cabbage is really limp. However, nutritionally speaking, the less the cabbage is cooked, the better. Try cooking for no more than 30 minutes. Bohemian Red Cabbage is particularly well accompanied by a portion of game, such as venison or pheasant.

1 red cabbage (about 2 pounds), thinly shredded
1 tablespoon olive oil
1 medium red onion (about 5 ounces), thinly chopped
2 tablespoons caraway seeds
1/2 cup balsamic vinegar
1 1/2 tablespoons xylitol, or to taste
1 teaspoon allspice
1 green apple, unpeeled and grated
salt to taste
freshly ground black pepper, to taste

1. Steam the cabbage in your steamer for about 10 minutes. Drain and set aside.
2. Meanwhile heat the oil in a large saucepan and sauté the onion until soft and translucent, but not brown.
3. Add the caraway seeds and sauté briefly. Stir in the vinegar, xylitol and allspice and sauté for another 2 minutes.
4. Mix in the grated apple.
5. Add the cabbage. Season with salt and pepper to taste. Stir thoroughly, to coat the cabbage evenly with all the ingredients.
6. Cover and bring slowly to a boil. Simmer on very low heat for 20-30 minutes, stirring once in a while, to avoid the cabbage sticking to the pan.
7. Adjust the seasoning, if necessary, and check for doneness. The cabbage should be very tender and soft.

Vegetable Dishes
Bok Choy with Mushrooms
Yield: 2 servings

A tasty and interesting way to prepare the super vegetable, bok choy.
This dish is prepared entirely in the microwave oven.

1 pound bok choy
2 cups oyster mushrooms (about 5 ounces), cleaned
1/2 teaspoon sesame oil
1 tablespoon light soy sauce
1 tablespoon oyster sauce
1 tablespoon sesame seeds

1. Coarsely shred the leaves of the bok choy. Cut the trimmed stems in half lengthways. Rinse separately under cold water.
2. Place bok choy stems around the edge of a large shallow microwave-safe dish. Place leaves in the center. No need to add water, as there is enough left from the rinsing process.
3. Cover and cook in the microwave oven at high power (about 650 Watt) for about 5 minutes, stirring halfway through. Stems should be just tender.
4. Drain in a large colander, until there is no liquid left. Set aside.
5. Meanwhile prepare the mushrooms, by cutting the large ones in half. Mix the remaining ingredients in a small bowl and combine with the mushrooms. Place them in the microwave-safe dish.
6. Cover and cook at high power (about 650 Watt) for about 3 minutes, or until the mushrooms are done, stirring halfway through.
7. Stir in the bok choy and cook, covered, for 1 minute, or until heated through.

Vegetable Dishes
Broccoli Gratin
Yield: 4 servings

This is an easy to prepare dish, full of healthy vegetables.

2 pounds broccoli florets, fresh or frozen
olive oil spray
4 medium tomatoes (about 1 pound)
2 large onions (about 3/4 pound), thinly sliced
salt to taste
ground black pepper, to taste
4 eggs, omega-3
2 tablespoons water
1 teaspoon dried thyme
1 tablespoon grated Parmesan cheese (the purist will leave it out)

1. Cook the broccoli florets in slightly salted, boiling water for approximately 3 minutes. The broccoli should still be very firm. Drain in a colander.
2. Spray a large, table-ready baking dish with the olive oil and lay out the broccoli florets on the bottom.
3. Meanwhile place the tomatoes in a bowl and pour boiling water over them. Set aside for one minute. Drain, slip the skins off, quarter, seed and chop roughly. Set aside in a colander.
4. Spray a frying pan with the olive oil and sauté the onion, until soft and translucent, but not brown.
5. Lay out the onion amongst the broccoli florets in the baking dish. Place the tomato in between the vegetables. Salt and pepper to taste.
6. Beat the eggs and water with a hand-whisk in a small mixing bowl. Salt and pepper to taste. Mix in the thyme.
7. Pour the eggs evenly over the vegetables. Sprinkle the cheese over the top (the purist will leave it out).
8. Bake in a hot oven at 340°F (170°C) for approximately 35 minutes. Check for doneness.

Vegetable Dishes
Broccoli Loaf
Yield: 4 servings

This dish is delicious served either hot or cold. The little bit of cheese is a slight lapse and the purist can leave it out.

1 pound frozen broccoli florets
olive oil spray
2 cloves garlic, crushed
4 tablespoons vegetable broth, or vegetable juice
salt to taste
ground black pepper, to taste
3 eggs, omega-3
1 tablespoon olive oil
1 pinch nutmeg
4-6 drops Tabasco sauce, or more to taste
1 tablespoon grated Swiss cheese (the purist will leave it out)

1. Take two florets of broccoli and set aside for decoration.
2. Spray a medium-size frying pan with the olive oil and sauté the rest of the broccoli rapidly.
3. Add the garlic and vegetable broth (or juice). Salt and pepper to taste. Sauté for a few minutes. The broccoli should stay crunchy.
4. Spray a table-ready loaf mold (say, 8.5 inches long, 4 inches wide, 3 inches high) with the olive oil and spread out the broccoli on the bottom.
5. In a medium-size mixing bowl, and using a hand-whisk, beat the eggs with the olive oil, nutmeg, Tabasco sauce and salt and pepper to taste. Stir in the cheese with a fork (the purist will leave it out).
6. Pour the mixture over the broccoli in the mold. Carefully press the broccoli down into the liquid to expel air and to keep it, as much as possible, under the surface of the liquid.
7. Bake in a hot oven at 340°F (170°C) for about 35 minutes. Check the eggs for doneness.

Vegetable Dishes
Broccoli Quiche
Yield: up to 8 servings

In the early days we thought that we would have to give up dishes, based on pastry. Now with the discovery of how to do them safely, we are delighted that we can now make a proper conforming quiche.

This dish will be popular with everybody. It's one of our favorites.

3/4 pound fresh broccoli
3 eggs, omega 3
6-8 tablespoons homemade Tomato Sauce Provençale (see page 31)*
2 pinches nutmeg
5-10 drops Tabasco sauce, or to taste
salt to taste
ground black pepper to taste
2 tablespoons chopped fresh parsley
olive oil spray
optional: 3 tablespoons grated Swiss cheese (the purist will leave it out)
Dough: (can be replaced by 'Savory Paleo Crust', see page 56)
2 eggs, omega 3
3 tablespoons olive oil
1 tablespoon red wine vinegar
1/4 baking powder
1/4 teaspoon salt
1 cup almond flour (about 3.5 ounces)
2 tablespoons coconut flour
3 tablespoons flax seed flour
2 tablespoons chia seeds (or sesame seeds)

1. Cut the cleaned broccoli into small bite-size florets. Steam for about 5 minutes. The broccoli should stay crunchy. Set aside.
2. Meanwhile beat the eggs with an electric hand mixer in a medium-size mixing bowl. Stir in the tomato sauce, enough to obtain the desired thickness. Season with nutmeg, Tabasco sauce and salt and pepper to taste.

3. Combine the egg-mixture with the broccoli and parsley. Set aside.

4. To prepare the dough, beat the eggs in a medium-size mixing bowl with an electric hand-mixer. Blend in all the other dough ingredients, until you obtain a pastry of thick consistency.

5. Spray a round, table-ready baking dish (about 10 inches diameter) with the olive oil and, by patting with a small spatula, spread out the dough, leaving a rim around the edge of about 1 inch high. Prick the bottom of the dough with a fork. Bake in a hot oven at 340°F (170°C) for about 8 minutes, until the dough is set.

6. Fill with the broccoli-egg mixture and bake for another 25 minutes, or until the eggs are cooked and the crust golden brown.

Optional: if you choose the version with the grated cheese (the purist will leave it out), you need to take the dish out of the oven after 15 minutes and sprinkle the cheese over the top of the dish. Return to the oven and bake until done.

7. Serve in the baking dish.

* Can be replaced by a thick ready-made marinara sauce.

Vegetable Dishes
Brussels Sprouts Gratin
Yield: 4 servings (as a main dish)

An excellent way to make an unexpectedly tasty dish out of Brussels sprouts.

This is a complete meal in itself and ideal as a main dish. It is very healthful too, both cauliflower and Brussels sprouts being 'super vegetables', and the eggs providing a good fatty acid balance.

2 pounds frozen Brussels sprouts
olive oil spray
4 eggs, omega-3
2 pinches nutmeg
2 cups (about 1 pound) 'Mock Mashed Potato Purée', homemade (see recipe page 92)
6 tablespoons vegetable broth, or vegetable juice
2 cloves garlic, crushed
2 tablespoons Parmesan cheese (the purist will leave it out)
salt to taste
ground black pepper to taste
5-10 drops Tabasco sauce, to taste

1. Defrost and cook the Brussels sprouts, following the instructions on the packet. Drain and chop roughly.
2. Spray a large, table-ready baking dish with the olive oil and spread out the Brussels sprouts on the bottom.
3. Meanwhile beat the eggs and nutmeg with an electric hand mixer in a medium-size mixing bowl. Mix in the 'Mock Mashed Potato Purée', the vegetable broth, the garlic and 1 tablespoon of Parmesan cheese (the purist will leave it out). Season with salt, pepper and Tabasco sauce to taste.
4. Pour the egg mixture equally over the Brussels sprouts. Sprinkle the remaining cheese over the top of the dish.
5. Bake in a hot oven at 340°F (170°C) for about 25 minutes, or until the top of the dish is golden brown. Serve in the baking dish.

Vegetable Dishes
Cabbage Curry
Yield: up to 6 servings

Enjoy this succulent dish – an unusual and tasty way of preparing a great combination of cabbage, tomato and onion.

olive oil spray
2 medium onions (about 1/2 pound), thinly sliced
4 cloves garlic, crushed
1 teaspoon grated fresh ginger
1/2 green bell pepper (about 2 ounces), seeded and finely chopped
2 teaspoons mild curry powder, or to taste
1 teaspoon mustard seeds
1 1/2 – 2 pounds white cabbage, thinly shredded
4 Roma tomatoes (about 3/4 pound), unpeeled and roughly chopped
salt and pepper, to taste

1. Spray a large saucepan with the olive oil and sauté the onion, until soft and translucent, but not brown.
2. Add the garlic, ginger, green bell pepper, curry powder and mustard seeds. Sauté on low heat for 2 minutes.
3. Add the cabbage and sauté on medium-high heat for 3 minutes.
4. Mix in the tomatoes. Salt and pepper to taste and sauté briefly on high heat.
5. Reduce heat and simmer, covered, for about 10-15 minutes, or until the cabbage is cooked, but still crunchy.

'Quick-Fix' Variation (yield: 2 servings):
1 tablespoon olive oil
1 cup (about 6 ounces) frozen chopped white onion
1 teaspoon ready-made chopped garlic
1 teaspoon ground ginger
1 teaspoon mild curry powder
1/2 teaspoon mustard seeds
1 'Ready Pack' (12 ounces) 'Angel Hair Coleslaw'
14-ounce can chopped tomatoes, drained
salt and ground black pepper, to taste

Vegetable Dishes
Carrots in Cumin
Yield: up to 6 servings

This is a creative way of using flavors and herbs to add zest to the common-or-garden carrot. This is a salt-free dish, but keep in mind that cooked carrots are glycemic. Be reasonable.

2 pounds carrots, peeled and sliced
2 tablespoons cumin seeds
2 tablespoons olive oil
freshly ground black pepper, to taste
2 teaspoons lemon juice
3 tablespoons chopped fresh parsley

1. Heat a large frying pan without any oil. Add the carrots and sauté on high heat for a few minutes, stirring all the time, until the carrots start to brown a bit. Turn down the heat.
2. On medium heat add the cumin seeds, the olive oil and pepper to taste. Toss well to coat the carrots and cook, stirring frequently for about 15-20 minutes (the cooking time is variable, depending on the quality of the carrots).
3. Check for doneness. Mix in the lemon juice.
4. Prior to serving, mix in the parsley and heat through.

Vegetable Dishes
Cauliflower Bake
Yield: 4 servings

Cauliflower is one of the 'super' vegetables and this recipe is a fine way to prepare it. It also includes lashings of onion and mushroom. Traditionally this dish is garnished with melted cheese (the purist will leave it out).

1 pound cauliflower florets , fresh or frozen
olive oil spray
salt to taste
freshly ground black pepper, to taste
1 big onion (about 7 ounces), sliced
2 cloves garlic, crushed
about 1/2 pound sliced mushrooms
4 eggs, omega-3
4 tablespoons vegetable broth, or vegetable juice
2 pinches nutmeg, or to taste
optional: 2 tablespoons grated Parmesan cheese (the purist will leave it out)

1. Steam or microwave the cauliflower florets, but stop when it is still crunchy. Drain in a colander.
2. Spray a large, table-ready baking dish with the oil and spread out the florets. Salt and pepper to taste. Set aside.
3. Meanwhile spray a nonstick frying pan with the oil and sauté the onion, until it is soft and translucent, but not brown.
4. Add the garlic. Mix in the mushrooms and sauté on medium-high heat, stirring constantly all the time, until they release their juices. Salt and pepper to taste.
5. Add the mushroom mixture to the baking dish and arrange to fill the spaces in between the cauliflower florets.
6. In a medium-size mixing bowl beat the eggs with a hand-whisk, together with the vegetable broth, the nutmeg and salt and pepper to taste. Pour egg mixture evenly over the vegetables in the baking dish.
7. Optional: sprinkle the Parmesan cheese over the top of the dish (the purist will leave it out).
8. Bake in a hot oven at 340°F (170°C) for around 25 minutes (or until the top of the dish is golden brown).

Vegetable Dishes
Cauliflower Risotto
Yield: 4 servings (as a main dish)

Sounds like a contradiction – a rice-free risotto!
Here the finely chopped cauliflower gives the same look, feel and taste of a classic risotto. This dish has lashings of wonderful vegetables and herbs too. Eat as much as you like!

4 cloves garlic
1 medium onion (about 4 ounces), quartered
olive oil spray
2 celery stalks (about 2 ounces), roughly sliced
1 green bell pepper (about 5 ounces), seeded and quartered
1 red bell pepper (about 7 ounces), seeded and quartered
5 green onions, finely chopped
1 cauliflower head (about 1 1/2 pounds), roughly cut in pieces
1 bay leave
1 1/2 teaspoons dried thyme
1/2 teaspoon ground cumin
1/2 teaspoon Sambal Oelek (or 10 drops Tabasco sauce), or to taste
2 cups (about 1/2 liter) chicken broth
ground black pepper to taste

1. Chop the garlic and onion in a food processor, using the blade.
2. Spray a large frying pan with the oil. Transfer the garlic and onion to the heated frying pan and sauté until soft.
3. Meanwhile chop the celery, green and red bell pepper (each of the items separately) in the food processor, using the blade. Transfer to the frying pan.
4. Add also the green onions and sauté all together for about 10 minutes.
5. Meanwhile chop the cauliflower in your food processor (using the blade) to the grainy texture of rice. Add to the vegetable mixture in the pan.
6. Stir in the bay leaf, thyme, cumin and Sambal Oelek to taste. Add the chicken broth and pepper to taste. Bring to a boil.
7. Reduce heat, cover and simmer for about 30 minutes. Stir a few times and cook uncovered for the last 5 minutes. The liquid should be evaporated and the cauliflower still be crunchy.

Vegetable Dishes
Eggplant and Tahini Pie
Yield: up to 8 servings

An interesting way to make an appetizing and unusual dish of eggplant.

2-3 large eggplants (about 2 pounds)
1 cup thick, ready-made tomato sauce (about 8 ounces)
1 tablespoon lemon juice
3/4 cup (about 6 ounces) ready-made sesame paste, also called 'tahini'
4 cloves garlic, crushed
2 tablespoons olive oil
2 tablespoons light soy sauce
Tabasco sauce, to taste
2 eggs, omega-3
2 tablespoons chopped fresh basil
ground black pepper, to taste

olive oil spray
garnish: 8 cherry tomatoes, cut in half

1. Prick the eggplants all over with a fork and roast them in a hot oven at 350°F (175°C) for around 55 minutes, turning them once (the eggplant flesh should be soft in the middle). Set aside to cool.
2. Peel the eggplants and place in a food processor. Add all the ingredients and blend to a smooth consistency.
3. Spray a table-ready baking-dish (about 10-inches diameter) with the olive oil and fill with the mixture. Spray the top of the pie lightly with the olive oil.
4. Bake for around 25 minutes in a hot oven at 340°F (170°C).
5. Take the dish out of the oven and decorate with the cherry tomato halves (cut-side upwards) and bake for another 20 minutes. Check for doneness.
6. Serve in the dish.

Vegetable Dishes
Eggplant and Tomato Medallions
Yield: 4 servings

This is a surprisingly complete and filling dish which can be eaten as part of a main meal – or is good for buffets or party snacks. The cheese option of course improves the look and eating experience, but is a significant lapse.

2 large eggplants (about 1 1/2 pounds), unpeeled
3 large, ripe, juicy tomatoes (about 1 1/2 pounds)
olive oil spray
salt to taste
freshly ground black pepper, to taste
2-3 teaspoons Italian seasoning, to taste
4 large cloves garlic, crushed
2 tablespoons chopped fresh basil
2 tablespoons olive oil
optional: about 12 ounces Mozzarella cheese (the purist will leave it out)

1. Cut the unpeeled eggplant in slices of about 1/2-inch. You should obtain about 16-20 slices.
2. Cut the tomatoes in slices of same thickness as the eggplant (there should be at least the same number of tomato slices).
3. Spray a baking tray or large baking dish with the olive oil and lay out the eggplant slices on the bottom. Salt and pepper to taste. Sprinkle half of the Italian seasoning over the top.
4. Place tomato slices on top of the eggplant slices (they should be covered entirely by the tomatoes). Salt and pepper to taste. Distribute the garlic evenly over the tomatoes. Sprinkle the remaining Italian seasoning, the basil, and finally the olive oil evenly over the tomatoes.
5. Bake in a hot oven at 340°F (170°C) for approximately 40 minutes, or until the eggplant is soft and done (depends on the variety of eggplants).
6. Optional (the purist will leave it out): cut the Mozzarella cheese into thin slices and cover the top of the cooked eggplant and tomato medallions. Put the dish back in the oven for 3 minutes, or until the cheese is melted.

Vegetable Dishes
Eggplant Stuffed
Yield: up to 4 servings as a side dish

Here we transform bland eggplant into a highly flavored and attractive meal.

olive oil spray
1 medium onion (around 5 ounces), chopped
14-ounce can chopped tomatoes
salt and pepper, to taste
2 large eggplants (about 2 pounds)
3 gloves garlic
4 twigs fresh parsley
1 tablespoon almond flour
1/4 teaspoon nutmeg
2 teaspoons crushed coriander seeds
1 teaspoon ground cinnamon
1 teaspoon xylitol
optional: grated Swiss cheese (the purist will leave it out)

1. Spray a frying pan with the olive oil and sauté the onion until soft and translucent, but not brown.
2. Add the chopped tomatoes. Cook uncovered over medium heat. When most of the liquid has evaporated, reduce the heat. Simmer, uncovered, stirring frequently, until the tomatoes start to stick to the pan. Salt and pepper to taste.
3. Meanwhile cut each eggplant in 2 halves. Scoop out the flesh, using a knife and a spoon, leaving a thin layer of flesh close to the skin. Set aside the flesh.
4. Pre-cook eggplant halves at 340°F (170°C) for 25 minutes.
5. Meanwhile cut the eggplant flesh roughly and combine in your food processor, together with the coarsely cut garlic and parsley. Using the blade, mix to obtain a fine consistency.
6. Add the mixture to the tomato sauce in the pan. Salt and pepper to taste. Stir in the almond flour. Season with nutmeg, coriander seeds, cinnamon and xylitol.
7. Fill the eggplant halves with the tomato mixture and lay out in an oiled, table-ready baking dish.
8. Bake in a hot oven at 340°F (170°C) for around 20 minutes.
9. Optional: sprinkle cheese over the eggplant halves and bake until melted (the purist will leave it out). Check for doneness.

Vegetable Dishes
Emma's Ratatouille
Yield: 4 servings

Ratatouille is a traditional vegetable dish from the South of France. This recipe was perfected by my daughter Emmanuelle Moranval, a Bond Precept follower, living in Briançon in the French Alps.
With the left-overs you can make a great vegetable omelet.

1 tablespoon olive oil
2 medium red onions (about 10 ounces), thinly sliced
4 large cloves garlic, crushed
3 tablespoons tomato paste
2 teaspoons Italian seasoning
1/2 teaspoon chili sauce, e.g. sambal oelek
1 pound fresh tomatoes, seeded and roughly chopped
1 pound eggplant, unpeeled and cut into 1-inch cubes
salt, to taste
ground black pepper, to taste
1 pound red bell peppers, seeded and cut into 1-inch strips
2 medium zucchini (about 3/4 pound), unpeeled and cut into 1/2-inch slices

1. Heat the oil in a large pot and sauté the onion, until soft and translucent, but not brown. Add the garlic and sauté shortly.
2. Mix in the tomato paste, the Italian seasoning and the chili sauce to taste.
3. Add the tomatoes and sauté for about 10 minutes.
4. Mix in the eggplant and salt and pepper to taste. Sauté for another 10 minutes.
5. Add the peppers and zucchini to the pot. Salt and pepper to taste.
6. Simmer covered for about 25 minutes, or until all the vegetables are cooked.

Vegetable Dishes
Fennel Casablanca
Yield: 2 servings

This is a different, unusual way of preparing Fennel, taking its inspiration from the flavors of Moroccan cuisine.

2 medium fennel bulbs (about 1 pound)
1 tablespoon lemon juice
3 tablespoons raisins
1 tablespoon olive oil
2 red onions (about 1/2 pound), thinly sliced
1/4 teaspoon freshly ground cumin
1/4 teaspoon freshly ground coriander
salt to taste
freshly ground black pepper, to taste
1/2 cup pine nuts, or slivered almonds (about 2 ounces)

1. Trim the green fronds from the fennel bulb and save for garnish. Clean the fennel bulbs, remove the stringy parts (as with celery). Cut each bulb in half and then cut in thin slices. Place the fennel in a bowl. Cover with water. Add the lemon juice. Prior to cooking, drain the fennel in a colander. Set aside to dry.
2. Meanwhile soak the raisins in hot water for 5 minutes. Drain and set aside.
3. Heat the oil in a medium-size frying pan and sauté the onion, until soft and translucent, but not brown.
4. Add the fennel slices to the onion and sauté on medium heat for about 5 minutes, stirring frequently. Season with the cumin, coriander, salt and pepper to taste. Cover and simmer until done, but still crunchy (the cooking time is very variable, depending on the quality of the vegetable).
5. Mix in the raisins and pine nuts and sauté briefly all together.
6. Prior to serving, chop the fennel fronds and sprinkle them as garnish over the dish.

Vegetable Dishes
Fennel Sautéed in Cumin Seeds
Yield: 2 servings

Fennel is often thought of as just a flavoring for other dishes. Here you find that it makes a fine dish in its own right.

2 medium fennel bulbs (about 1 pound)
1 tablespoon fresh lemon juice
olive oil spray
1 teaspoon cumin seeds
salt, to taste
freshly ground black pepper, to taste
1 tablespoon lime juice, or to taste

1. Trim the green fronds from the fennel bulb and save for garnish. Clean the fennel bulbs, remove the stalks and the stringy parts (as with celery). Cut each bulb in half. Cut each half in three. Place the fennel in a bowl. Cover with water. Add the lemon juice.
2. Prior to cooking, drain the fennel in a colander. Dry each fennel piece with kitchen paper.
3. Spray a medium-size frying pan with the olive oil and sauté the fennel rapidly on both sides, stirring frequently, for about 5 minutes.
4. Mix in the cumin seeds and salt and pepper to taste. Cover and simmer until the fennel is done, but still crunchy (the cooking time is very variable, depending on the quality of the vegetable).
5. Mix in the lime juice to taste.
6. Prior to serving, chop the fennel fronds and sprinkle them as garnish over the dish.

Vegetable Dishes
Green Beans with Tomato
Yield: 4 servings as a side dish

This is a tasty and fully conforming plant food dish. Consume as much as you fancy.

4 medium tomatoes (about 1 1/2 pounds)
olive oil spray
2 medium red onion (about 1/2 pound), chopped
4 cloves garlic, crushed
1/2 cup vegetable broth, or vegetable juice
ground black pepper, to taste
optional: 1 teaspoon dried rosemary, or to taste
1 pound green beans, fresh or frozen
2 tablespoons chopped fresh parsley

1. Place the tomatoes in a medium-size bowl and pour boiling water over them. Set aside for 1 minute. Then drain the tomatoes, peel off the skin, cut in quarters, seed and chop them roughly. Set aside.
2. Spray a large frying pan with the olive oil and sauté the onion, until soft and translucent, but not brown. Stir in the garlic and the tomatoes. Sauté for another 2 minutes.
3. Add the vegetable broth. Season with pepper and rosemary (optional) to taste.
4. Bring to a boil. Add the green beans to the tomatoes and simmer, covered, until the green beans are cooked, but still green and crunchy.
5. Drain excess liquid, if any. Mix in the parsley and serve.

Vegetable Dishes
Mock Mashed Potato Purée
Yield: up to 4 servings as a side dish

This is a purée that is intended to be eaten just as it is – it closely resembles mashed potato. Your unsuspecting guests will not be able to tell the difference! But of course it has all the advantages of the 'super-vegetable' cauliflower – and none of the drawbacks of potato. It is also a wonderful, healthful product for thickening soups and sauces. You thus avoid the use of flour and other undesirable, bad carbohydrate thickeners.

1 pound cauliflower florets, fresh or frozen
1 small white onion (about 3 ounces), quartered
2 tablespoons olive oil
1/2 teaspoon salt
ground black pepper, to taste
2 pinches of nutmeg, or to taste
only if needed: 1-2 tablespoons vegetable broth, or vegetable juice
optional: 4-ounce can chopped black olives

1. Steam the cauliflower florets, together with the onion, until tender.
2. Place the vegetables in a food processor, together with the oil, salt, pepper and nutmeg to taste. Blend to obtain a smooth consistency. Depending on the quality of the cauliflower, you might need more liquid to obtain this result. Hence add a little vegetable broth (or juice) if needed.
3. Optional: if you want to serve the mock mashed potato purée as a side dish (and not use it as a thickener), you may choose to mix in the chopped olives.

Vegetable Dishes
Multicolored Gratin
Yield: 6 servings as a side dish

This is a fine, high plant-food dish and looks quite impressive on your table with its alternating colors.

3 medium white onions (about 1 pound), thinly sliced
olive oil spray
2-3 zucchini (about 3/4 pound)
3-4 ripe tomatoes (about 1 1/4 pound)
salt, to taste
ground black pepper, to taste
5 cloves garlic, crushed
2 teaspoons thyme, fresh or dried, to taste

1. Spray a medium-size frying pan with the olive oil and sauté the onion, until soft and translucent, but not brown.
2. Spray a table-ready baking dish (say, 13x9 inches) with the olive oil and cover the bottom with the onion.
3. Meanwhile cut the unpeeled zucchini into slices and set aside. Slice the tomatoes to the same thickness as the zucchini and set aside.
4. Place on top of the onion layer in the dish the zucchini and tomato slices in alternating straight rows, so as to obtain red and green alternating colors.
5. Sprinkle with salt and pepper to taste. Distribute the garlic and thyme equally over the vegetables. Spray olive oil equally over the vegetables.
6. Bake in a preheated oven at 340°F (170°C) for about 50 minutes, tamping the vegetables from time to time with the back of a serving spoon. The vegetables should be slightly caramelized. Check for doneness.
7. This dish can be savored either hot or cold. Serve in the dish.

Vegetable Dishes
Nicole's Pizza
Yield: 4 servings

This is a dish containing a good balance of vegetation and proteins of various kinds. The 'Pizza Crust' in this recipe (page 55) is of course fully conforming. It is popular with the kids too!

olive oil spray
1 medium onion (about 5 ounces), chopped
2 cloves garlic, crushed
1 teaspoon Italian Seasoning
14-ounce can chopped tomatoes
salt to taste
ground black pepper, to taste
2 tablespoons chopped fresh parsley
1 1/2 tablespoon Dijon mustard
1 'Pizza Crust' (see page 55), pre-baked
optional: 2 small tomatoes (about 7 ounces), cut in 1/4-inch slices
2 tablespoons grated Parmesan cheese (not for the purist!)

1. Spray a medium-size frying pan with the olive oil and sauté the onion until soft and translucent, but not brown.
2. Stir in the garlic and the Italian seasoning. Add the tomatoes and salt and pepper to taste.
3. Cook over medium heat, uncovered, stirring frequently, until you obtain a tomato sauce of thick consistency (the cooking process will take up to 30 minutes). Mix in the parsley. Set aside.
4. Spread the mustard in a thin layer over the pre-baked 'Pizza Crust', using a small spatula. Distribute the tomato sauce evenly on top. Optional: lay out the tomato slices in a circle on top.
5. Bake in a hot oven at 340°F (170°C) for about 20 minutes. If you have chosen to add the tomato slices (optional) to the dish, you will need to add about 5 more minutes to the baking time.
6. If you choose the optional version with the Parmesan cheese (the purist will leave it out), you need to take the dish out of the oven about 5 minutes before the end of the baking time and sprinkle the Parmesan cheese over the top of the dish. Bake until the cheese is melted – which may take a few minutes.

Vegetable Dishes
Oriental Zucchini Quick-Fix
Yield: 4 servings as a side dish

A curry is often a good way to spice up bland veggies (like zucchini). Here, by the judicious use of other eastern spices and condiments, we conjure up a dish redolent of the orient. Since this is a quick fix, we focus on the use of several ready-prepared ingredients, but nothing stops you from substituting fresh.

This dish tastes its best the day after its preparation.

olive oil spray
1 cup frozen chopped onion (about 4 ounces)
2 teaspoons ready-made chopped garlic
1 teaspoon ready-made chopped ginger
2-3 teaspoons red curry paste (Thai or similar mild), to taste
1/2 cup coconut milk
2 teaspoons light soy sauce
2 pounds zucchini, unpeeled and cut into bite-size pieces
2 teaspoons lemon juice
ground black pepper, to taste

1. Spray a large frying pan (or wok) with the oil and sauté the onion, until soft and translucent, but not brown.
2. Mix in the garlic and ginger. Sauté all together for 2 minutes.
3. Blend in the curry paste to taste, the coconut milk and soy sauce.
4. Add the zucchini to the pan and coat with the sauce.
5. Cover and bring slowly to a boil. Simmer for about 30 minutes, or until the zucchini are done.
6. Season with the lemon juice and pepper to taste.

Vegetable Dishes
Peperonata Provençale
Yield: 4 servings

Peperonata is an Italian stew of slow cooked bell peppers with onions and tomatoes. It is often eaten as a side dish.
In the South of France we used to add eggs to ratatouille to make a nourishing and satisfying main dish. Here we have done the same for Peperonata.

olive oil spray
2 medium onion (about 10 ounces), chopped
2 pounds green bell peppers, quartered, seeded and cut into 1-inch strips
28-ounce can chopped tomatoes
4 cloves garlic, crushed
2 teaspoons Herbs of Provence
1/2 teaspoon xylitol
salt, to taste
ground black pepper to taste
4 eggs, omega-3

1. Spray a large frying pan (or saucepan) with the olive oil and sauté the onion until soft and translucent, but not brown.
2. Add the bell peppers and continue to cook, stirring frequently until they wilt.
3. Mix in the tomatoes, the garlic, the Herbs of Provence and the xylitol. Season with salt and pepper to taste.
4. Cook uncovered over medium heat. When most of the liquid has evaporated, reduce the heat. Simmer, uncovered, stirring frequently. This whole process may take approximately up to 45 minutes, or until the tomatoes start to stick to the pan.
5. Lightly beat the eggs with a fork and empty them into the pan over the vegetables, stirring until the entire mixture sets.

Vegetable Dishes
Quick Roasted Veggies
Yield: 4 servings as a side dish

A magnificent, colorful and tasty vegetable dish that is quickly put together - and that all the family can enjoy. It is a quicker, simpler version of Roasted Summer Vegetables, see page 98.

olive oil spray
2 medium red onions (about 10 ounces), cut through the root into four quarters, and then each quarter into half
1 big eggplant (about 1 pound), peeled and cut into 1-inch cubes
2 red bell peppers (about 3/4 pound), seeded and cut into 1-inch strips
4 large cloves garlic
2 teaspoons Italian seasoning
2 tablespoons olive oil
salt, to taste
freshly ground black pepper, to taste

1. Spray a large, table-ready baking dish with the olive oil and spread out the onion, eggplant and bell pepper randomly.
2. Cut the garlic cloves in slices and distribute equally amongst the vegetables.
3. Sprinkle the vegetables with the Italian seasoning and with the olive oil. Salt and pepper to taste (mix with your hands to ensure the vegetables are fully covered).
4. Bake in a hot oven at 340°F (170°C) for about 40 minutes, then cover with an aluminum foil and bake for another 15 minutes, or until the vegetables are done.

Vegetable Dishes
Roasted Summer Vegetables
Yield: up to 6 servings

This is a hearty and varied vegetable dish. It is quite filling and can easily serve as a complete meal in itself. Note the baked garlic bulb. This is a little-known but delicious way of eating garlic. It is possible to bake garlic on its own as a side dish.

2 medium red onions
2 medium red bell peppers
2 large garlic bulbs
2 Japanese eggplants (small eggplants)
2 medium zucchini
2 medium tomatoes
1 small squash
8 button mushrooms
olive oil spray
1/4 cup olive oil
1/4 cup vegetable broth, or vegetable juice
2 teaspoons dried thyme
salt (moderate), to taste
ground black pepper, to taste

1. Peel and quarter the onions. Pre-cook for 3 minutes, by microwaving them at high power (650 Watt). Set aside.
2. Halve and seed the peppers, removing the stalks and any white membrane. Cut each pepper into quarters. Set aside.
3. With a sharp knife cut the cleaned, but unpeeled garlic bulbs in half through the equator. Set aside.
4. Cut the calyxes off the unpeeled eggplants and unpeeled zucchini. Cut both vegetables in half lengthwise. Set aside.
5. Cut the tomatoes in half through the equator. Set aside.
6. Take the unpeeled squash and cut off any stalk. Cut into 8 slices. Set aside.
7. Clean the mushrooms gently with a kitchen paper and cut off the ends of the stalks. Set aside.
8. Spray a very large, table-ready baking dish with the olive oil and distribute the vegetables (cut-side up), so that their colors make an attractive presentation.

Vegetable Dishes

9. Mix the olive oil with the vegetable broth and pour equally over the vegetables. Season with thyme, salt and pepper to taste.

10. Cover the dish with an aluminum foil and bake in a preheated oven at 340°F (170°C) for about 30 minutes.

11. Take off the foil and bake uncovered for another 25-30 minutes. The vegetables should be tender and browning but not disintegrating. The garlic (still in its husk) should be golden and soft. Check the vegetables for doneness.

Spicy Eggplant Quick-Fix
Yield: 4 servings

This dish is quite quickly knocked together, using eggplant and ingredients commonly found in the kitchen.

It mellows and takes its full flavor the day after preparation.

The use of hot condiment (curry) is not aggressive: the quantities are modest, just enough to give zing to the bland eggplant.

olive oil spray
3 medium eggplants (about 1 3/4 pound), unpeeled and cut into bite-size pieces
2 medium red onions (about 10 ounces), sliced
2 tablespoons red Thai curry paste (Thai or similar mild)
1 tablespoon light soy sauce
14-ounce can chopped tomatoes
ground black pepper, to taste
optional: 3 twigs fresh basil

1. Spray a large frying pan (or wok) with the olive oil and sauté the eggplant for about 5 minutes, stirring frequently.
2. Stir in the onion and sauté for another 2 minutes.
3. Mix in the curry paste and soy sauce and coat the eggplant evenly.
4. Add the tomatoes with their juice. Season with pepper to taste.
5. Bring slowly to a boil, then simmer covered for about 20-30 minutes, or until the eggplant is done.
6. Optional: prior to serving, garnish with the basil leaves.

Vegetable Dishes
Spinach Hash
Yield: up to 4 servings as a side dish

This is a dish that is quickly knocked up. You might be surprised by the choice of peanuts, but the raw, unsalted ones are tolerable, if you are not allergic to them. The purist can substitute them with chopped walnuts instead.

olive oil spray
1 medium onion (about 5 ounces), chopped
2 cloves garlic, crushed
1 teaspoon paprika
2 tablespoons tomato paste
1 pound tomatoes, seeded and chopped
salt, to taste
ground black pepper, to taste
1 pound chopped frozen spinach
1/3 cup (about 1 1/2 ounces) chopped raw, unsalted peanuts

1. Spray a large frying pan with the olive oil and gently sauté the onion, until soft and translucent, but not brown.
2. Stir in the garlic and sauté for 2 minutes. Mix in the paprika and tomato paste.
3. Stir in the tomatoes and salt and pepper to taste. Simmer uncovered, stirring frequently, for about 15 minutes.
4. Meanwhile defrost the spinach, following the instructions on the packet.
5. Drain and add to the tomatoes and gently simmer until the vegetables are done. Adjust the seasoning, if necessary.
6. Mix in the peanuts towards the end of the cooking time and heat through.

Vegetable Dishes
Spinach Quiche
Yield: up to 8 servings

This simple recipe is a tasty way to prepare spinach – your kids will love it! It keeps well and can be served reheated or cold for that un-programmed snack.

2 cups sliced mushrooms (about 4 ounces)
1 tablespoon olive oil
2 cloves garlic, crushed
1 cup frozen chopped spinach, thawed and squeezed dry (about 8 ounces)
salt to taste
ground black pepper to taste
3 eggs, omega 3
2 pinches nutmeg
5-10 drops Tabasco sauce, or to taste
1 'Savory Paleo Crust' (see page 56), pre-baked
olive oil spray

1. Sauté the mushrooms in a non-stick frying pan, without any oil or water, on medium-high heat, stirring constantly all the time, until they release their juices. Stir in the oil, garlic and spinach and salt and pepper to taste.
2. Meanwhile beat the eggs with an electric hand mixer in a medium-size mixing bowl. Season with nutmeg, Tabasco sauce and salt and pepper to taste.
3. Fill the pre-baked crust in the baking dish with the spinach-egg mixture.
4. Bake in a hot oven at 340°F (170°C) for about 30 minutes, or until the eggs are cooked and the crust golden brown.

Vegetable Dishes
Spinach Roly-Poly
Yield: 6 servings as a starter – or 2 servings as a main dish

Thanks to Jeanne Bouvet of Annecy, France, for this delicious recipe. In spite of appearances, this recipe is remarkably easy to do, and your guests will admire you for your cookery skills!

1/2 pound fresh spinach leaves
4 eggs, omega-3
1/4 teaspoon nutmeg
1 teaspoon garlic powder
salt and pepper, to taste
optional: 4 slices of Mozzarella cheese (not for the purist!)

1. Wash the spinach and steam for about 4-5 minutes, or until the spinach is reduced and soft. Drain by pressing it in a sieve.
2. Let cool, then take the drained spinach in your hands and squeeze out all the liquid. You end up with a ball of spinach (about the size of a tennis ball), which you chop up. Set aside.
3. Meanwhile break the eggs and carefully separate the yolks from the whites into 2 separate mixing bowls.
4. Season the egg yolks with the nutmeg, garlic powder and salt and pepper to taste. Add the chopped spinach and, using a fork, coat with the yolks.
5. Beat the egg whites to a stiff consistency, using an electric hand-mixer. Using a spatula, fold the whites gently into the spinach-egg yolk mixture.
6. Line a baking tray with non-stick baking paper and, using a spatula, spread out the spinach and egg mixture into a rectangle of about 9x11 inches.
7. Bake in a hot oven at 320°F (160°C) for about 12-15 minutes. Check the eggs for doneness.
8. Optional: spread out the Mozzarella slices over the top of the bake and return to the oven for a few minutes, until the cheese is melted.
9. Take bake out of oven and slide the baking paper, with the spinach bake on it, gently sideways out of the baking tray. With the help of the paper, roll up the spinach bake into a roly-poly.
10. Serving suggestions: cut the roly-poly into thick slices and serve on individual plates on a bed of tomato coulis.

Vegetable Dishes
Stuffed Portabella Bake
Yield: 2-3 servings

A surprisingly simple dish to prepare. The end result is impressive. Food-wise this is a fine and nutritious dish.

olive oil spray
1 onion (about 5 ounces), chopped
2 cloves garlic, crushed
14-ounce can chopped tomatoes
1 teaspoon Italian seasoning
salt, to taste
ground black pepper, to taste
6 Portabella mushrooms (about 6 ounces)
10 ounces frozen chopped spinach
optional: 6 Mozzarella cheese slices (the purist will leave it out)

1. Spray a medium-size frying pan with the olive oil and sauté the onion, until soft and translucent, but not brown. Stir in the garlic and heat through.
2. Drain half of the juice from the tomatoes. Add then to the pan. Mix in the Italian seasoning, salt and pepper to taste and sauté for about 10 minutes.
3. Meanwhile clean the mushrooms gently with kitchen paper, but cut the stems. Set aside the mushrooms. Finely chop up the stems and add to the tomato mixture. Simmer uncovered for about 10 minutes.
4. Defrost the spinach in the microwave for about 3 minutes (or follow the instructions on the packet). Drain in a colander. Then mix into the tomato mixture in the frying pan, stirring all together. Adjust the seasoning with salt and pepper to taste.
5. Spray a table-ready, medium-size baking dish with the olive oil and cover the bottom with half of the sauce.
6. Distribute the Portabella mushrooms upside-down on the sauce and sprinkle lightly with pepper to taste.
7. Fill the mushrooms with the rest of the sauce.
8. Cover with aluminum foil and bake in a hot oven at 340°F (170°C) for about 20 minutes. Check mushrooms for doneness.
9. Optional (the purist will leave it out): cover the mushrooms with the cheese slices and place the dish under the grill for 2-3 minutes, or until the cheese is melted.

Vegetable Dishes
Vegetable Lasagna
Yield: about 6 servings (as a main dish)

This makes a fine plant-food dish with the vegetables layered in a tasty marinara sauce. It is like lasagna, but without the unwanted pasta.

1 1/2 pounds red bell peppers
salt, to taste
ground black pepper, to taste
6 sun-dried tomatoes
3/4 pound mushrooms, sliced
1 tablespoon olive oil
2 large cloves garlic, crushed
olive oil spray
3/4 pound red onions, sliced
1 jar (about 20 ounces) ready-made marinara sauce*
1 pound eggplant, unpeeled and thinly sliced
3 teaspoons Italian seasoning
3/4 pound zucchini, unpeeled and sliced
5 tablespoons red wine
optional: 3 tablespoons grated Parmesan cheese (the purist will leave it out)

1. Wash the bell peppers and bake in a preheated oven at 340°F (170°C) for about 40 minutes, turning them once. Their skin should be wrinkled. Place them in a plastic bag and close tightly. Allow to cool. It is now easy to remove the skin of the bell peppers. Cut them open and remove the seeds, stalks and ribs. Cut into 3-inch strips. Salt and pepper to taste. Set aside.
2. Pour boiling water over the sun-dried tomatoes and soak for 5 minutes. Drain, cut in small dices and set aside.
3. Meanwhile sauté the mushrooms in a hot, non-stick frying pan, no oil, stirring constantly, until they release their juices. Continue until all the liquid has evaporated. Mix in the tablespoon of olive oil and the garlic. Heat through and salt and pepper to taste. Set aside on a plate.
4. Spray the frying pan with the olive oil and sauté the onion, until soft and translucent, but not brown. Set aside.

Vegetable Dishes

5. Spray a large, table-ready baking dish (say, 14x10 inches) with the olive oil and cover the bottom with 1/3 of the marinara sauce.

6. Lay out the eggplant slices on top. Salt and pepper to taste. Sprinkle with 1 teaspoon of Italian seasoning.

Lay out the zucchini slices on top. Salt and pepper to taste. Sprinkle with another teaspoon of the Italian seasoning.

Cover with another 1/3 of the marinara sauce.

Lay out the bell pepper strips on top, followed by a layer of mushrooms and a layer of onion.

7. Mix the sun-dried tomatoes into the remaining marinara sauce and cover the top of the vegetables. Sprinkle with the remaining Italian seasoning.

8. Pour the wine equally over the dish and sprinkle with the cheese (optional-the purist will leave it out).

9. Bake in a preheated oven at 340°F (170°C) for about 1 hour, or until the vegetables are all done. In particular, check the eggplant for doneness.

* Choose a 'safe' one – read the ingredients list.

Vegetable Dishes
Vegetable Loaf
Yield: 6 servings

This recipe makes a tasty 'loaf' of vegetables. Eat a thick slice as a starter or part of a main meal. It is good as a party nibble too.

1 onion (about 6 ounces)
4 medium cloves garlic
1 carrot (about 4 ounces), peeled
1/2 green bell pepper (2-3 ounces)
3 celery stalks of about 6 inches long (about 4 ounces)
2 tablespoons fresh parsley, roughly chopped
1/4 cup chicken broth (or vegetable broth)
1 tablespoon light soy sauce
1 tablespoon olive oil
2 eggs, omega-3
1 1/2 cups almond flour (about 6 ounces)
2 tablespoons chia seeds
freshly ground black pepper, to taste
4-6 drops Tabasco sauce, to taste
olive oil spray

1. Quarter the onion, halve the garlic cloves and cut the carrot, green bell pepper and the celery stalks roughly into pieces and combine in the bowl of a food processor. Mix the vegetables, using the blade accessory.
2. Add the parsley, the chicken (or vegetable) broth, the soy sauce, the olive oil, the eggs and the almond flour and blend all together into a rough vegetable mixture.
3. Mix in the chia seeds. Season with pepper and Tabasco sauce to taste.
4. Spray a table-ready loaf mold (say, 9 inches long, 5 inches wide, 3 inches high) with olive oil and fill with the mixture.
5. Bake for about 50-55 minutes in a hot oven at 340°F (170°C). Check the center for doneness. Serve in the baking dish.

Vegetable Dishes
Vegetable Rissoles
Yield: up to 15 rissoles (2.5 – 3-inch diameter)

This is a tasty and interesting way of wrapping up vegetables in an attractive rissole. Children love it.

2 medium zucchini (about 1/2 pound), cut roughly into pieces
1 small carrot (about 3 ounces), peeled and roughly cut into pieces
1 medium red onion (about 4 ounces), quartered
2 cloves garlic
1 egg, omega-3
1 tablespoon almond flour
2-3 tablespoons nutritional yeast flakes, to taste
1/4 teaspoon salt, or to taste
ground black pepper, to taste
olive oil spray

1. Combine the zucchini, carrot, onion and garlic in a food processor and, using the blade, mix to obtain a coarse consistency. Transfer to a large mixing bowl.
2. Beat the egg and the almond flour with an electric hand mixer in a small mixing bowl, until smooth. Stir in the yeast flakes (to taste).
3. Add to the vegetable mixture in the large bowl. Mix with a fork until the veggies are coated with the egg mixture. Season with salt and pepper to taste.
4. Spray a large, non-stick frying pan with the oil and bring to medium-high heat.
5. Scoop rissole-size dollops of the vegetable mixture into the hot pan. With a spatula pat down each dollop and shape them into rissoles of about 2.5 – 3-inch diameter.
6. Sauté the rissoles from each side, until browned and crispy. Since they are fragile, use 2 spatulas to carefully turn them over. This may take about 8 minutes for each batch. Spray more oil in the pan between each batch and repeat until the vegetable mixture is used up.
7. Transfer the rissoles to a hot serving plate.

Vegetable Dishes
Winter Cabbage Stew
Yield: 2-3 servings

This hearty, chunky stew suits any time of year and is particularly welcome on a chilly evening. A great way to spice up that fine vegetable, cabbage.

1 tablespoon olive oil
1 medium onion (about 6 ounces), roughly chopped
2 medium celery stalks (about 4 ounces), sliced
3 sun-dried tomatoes, chopped
2 cloves garlic, crushed
2 tablespoons mild curry paste
14-ounce can chopped tomatoes
1/2 white cabbage (about 1 pound), chopped
1 1/2 cups vegetable broth, or vegetable juice
salt, to taste
ground black pepper, to taste

1. In a large saucepan heat the olive oil and sauté the onion, until soft and translucent, but not brown.
2. Add the celery, sun-dried tomatoes and garlic and sauté for 5 minutes.
3. Mix in the curry paste and allow the flavors to develop for 2 minutes.
4. Mix in the chopped tomatoes.
5. Add the cabbage and coat well with all the ingredients in the saucepan. Sauté, uncovered, for 5 minutes.
6. Add the vegetable broth (or juice). Season with salt and pepper to taste.
7. Cover and simmer for about 10-15 minutes, or until the cabbage is cooked, but still crunchy.

Vegetable Dishes
Zucchini Dug-Outs
Yield: up to 4 servings

It serves 2 people as a main dish or 4 people as a side dish.
The dug-out zucchini look like rustic native canoes piled high
with their delicious, colorful cargos. This dish can be served
either hot or cold.

2 pounds zucchini, unpeeled, cut lengthwise in 2 halves
salt, to taste
freshly ground black pepper, to taste
1 teaspoon dried Italian seasoning
olive oil spray
1 medium onion (about 5 ounces), chopped
4 cloves garlic, crushed
14-ounce can chopped tomatoes, drained
1 tablespoon tomato paste
2 pinches ground nutmeg
1/2 teaspoon xylitol, or to taste
4-6 drops Tabasco Sauce, or to taste
2 tablespoons crushed pine nuts
optional: 1 tablespoon grated Swiss cheese (the purist will leave
it out)
1 tablespoon chopped fresh parsley

1. Carefully scrape out the soft pulp of the zucchini halves with
a small spoon, so they take on the form of a dug-out canoe.
2. Take half of the pulp and chop it very thinly. Set aside
(dispose of the other half).
3. Lightly salt and pepper the zucchini halves and sprinkle with
half of the Italian seasoning.
4. Spray a baking tray with the olive oil and lay out the zucchini
halves.
5. Bake in a hot oven at 340°F (170°C) for about 25 minutes.
6. Meanwhile spray a medium-size frying pan with the oil and
sauté the onion, until soft and translucent, but not brown.
7. Stir in the garlic and the chopped zucchini pulp and sauté all
together for about 10 minutes.
8. Add the drained tomatoes, tomato paste and the rest of the
Italian seasoning. Season with nutmeg, xylitol, Tabasco sauce,
salt and pepper to taste. Sauté all together for 2 minutes.

Vegetable Dishes

9. Mix in the pine nuts.

10. Distribute the mixture equally in the hollowed-out zucchini halves on the baking sheet.

11. Optional: sprinkle the cheese over the top (the purist will leave it out).

12. Bake in the hot oven at 340°F (170°C) for about 30 minutes, or until the zucchini are done.

13. Prior to serving, sprinkle with the parsley.

Vegetable Dishes
Zucchini with Sun-dried Tomatoes
Yield: 4 servings as a side dish

A tasty and nutritious way of preparing zucchini. With the left-over you can also make a great vegetable omelet.

1/4 cup sun-dried tomatoes
olive oil spray
2 medium red onion (about 1/2 pound), thinly sliced
4 cloves garlic, crushed
2 teaspoons grated ginger
1/4 teaspoon chili sauce, or to taste
1/4 teaspoon ground cumin, or to taste
1/4 teaspoon ground coriander, or to taste
2 pounds zucchini, unpeeled, thinly sliced
salt to taste
ground black pepper, to taste
1 teaspoon lemon juice

1. Soak the sun-dried tomatoes in hot water for 5 minutes. Drain, but keep 1/2 cup of the liquid and set aside. Cut the drained sun-dried tomatoes in small pieces and set aside.
2. Spray a large saucepan with the olive oil and sauté the onion, until soft and translucent, but not brown.
3. Mix in the garlic and ginger and sauté for 2 minutes.
4. Season with the chili sauce, cumin and coriander to taste.
5. Mix in the sun-dried tomatoes, together with the 1/2 cup of their liquid.
6. Add the zucchini and salt and pepper to taste. Sauté for about 30 minutes, or until the zucchini are done.
7. Mix in the lemon juice.

CHAPTER 6
Poultry, Game & Meat

Baked Turkey Breast
Yield: up to 8 servings

In this recipe frozen turkey breast is used. Even better is the use of fresh turkey. Then you need to revise the baking time in the oven.

2 pounds frozen boneless turkey breast, thawed
olive oil spray
Marinade:
3 tablespoons olive oil
1 tablespoon light soy sauce
4 cloves garlic, crushed
2 teaspoons grated fresh ginger
freshly ground black pepper, to taste

1. Rinse the turkey breast in running water. Pat dry with kitchen paper and set aside.
2. Combine the marinade ingredients in a small mixing bowl.
3. Coat the turkey breast from both sides evenly with the marinade.
4. Spray a large baking dish with the olive oil and place the turkey breast on the bottom. Dispose the leftover from the marinade around.
5. Bake in a hot oven at 340°F (170°C) for around 1 hour. Check for doneness with a meat thermometer.

Poultry, Game & Meat
Bond Chicken Burgers
Yield: 8 burgers (3-inch diameter size)

You may wrap the burger in a piece of romaine lettuce and combine with, for example, mustard or your favorite salsa, or with another of your favorite condiments.

2-3 shallots (about 3 ounces)
3 cloves garlic
4 sprigs fresh parsley
2 eggs, omega-3
1 tablespoon olive oil
1/2 teaspoon salt, or to taste
freshly ground black pepper, to taste
a few drops of Tabasco sauce, to taste
1/2 cup almond flour (about 2 ounces)
1 pound ground chicken breast, skinless and fatless
olive oil spray

1. Combine shallots, garlic and parsley in a food processor and, using the blade, blend to obtain a finely chopped consistency. Set aside.
2. Beat the eggs and oil in a large mixing bowl with an electric hand-mixer. Salt and pepper to taste. Season with a few drops of Tabasco sauce to taste.
3. Mix in the almond flour. Add shallots, garlic and parsley.
4. Add the ground burger meat to the mixture. Stir in uniformly, using a fork (or better, use your hands).
5. Form the mixture into 3-inch diameter patties (or any size you wish to give them).
6. Spray a large, non-stick frying pan with the oil and sauté the burgers from both sides until golden brown. Check the center for doneness.

Poultry, Game & Meat
Chicken Breast in Tomato and Onion
Yield: 2 servings

This dish can be quickly knocked up when you have surprise guests for example. Try to use organic, free-range chicken breast.

olive oil spray
1 skinless and fatless chicken breast (about 1/2 pound), cut in half
salt to taste
freshly ground black pepper, to taste
1 large red onion (about 1/2 pound), coarsely sliced
4 large cloves garlic, sliced
2 teaspoons Italian seasoning
5 Roma tomatoes (about 1 pound), cut in halves
1 tablespoon chopped fresh parsley

1. Spray a large frying pan with the oil and sauté the chicken breast halves briefly on both sides, until golden brown. Salt and pepper to taste. Set aside on a plate and cover.
2. Spray some more oil in the pan and sauté the onion slices for about 5 minutes, stirring frequently and adding a little water, when they start to stick.
3. Stir in the garlic slices and 1 teaspoon of the Italian seasoning and sauté briefly.
4. Place the tomatoes, cut-side down, in the pan. Sauté for a few minutes, then turn on the other side. Salt and pepper to taste and sprinkle the remaining Italian seasoning over the tomatoes.
5. Sauté on medium heat for another few minutes. If the vegetables stick to the pan, add a little water.
6. Place the chicken breasts in the middle of the vegetables, cover and simmer for about 5-10 minutes. Check the chicken for doneness.
7. Prior to serving, mix in the parsley.

Chicken Korma
Yield: 6 servings

Inspired by the Indian cuisine I have created this tasty mild curry. Best prepared the day before. Serve with 'Mock Mashed Potato Purée' (see recipe page 92).

Marinade:

5 ounces raw cashew nuts
2 teaspoons curry powder
3 teaspoons ground coriander
1/2 teaspoon cayenne pepper, or to taste
4 cloves garlic, crushed
2 teaspoons grated ginger
2 tablespoons white wine vinegar
1 tablespoon tomato paste
3/4 cup coconut milk

2 pounds skinless chicken breast, cut into 1-inch cubes
olive oil spray
1 medium onion (about 5 ounces), finely chopped
2 teaspoons sweet paprika powder
3 cardamom pods
1 cinnamon stick
1 cup ready-made tomato purée
1 cup chicken broth
1 cup coconut milk

1. **Marinade:** place the cashews in a blender and grind into flour. Add the remaining marinade ingredients and blend until you obtain a creamy texture.
2. Place the chicken cubes in a large bowl and coat with the marinade. Cover and keep refrigerated overnight.
3. The next day, spray a large frying pan with the oil and sauté the onion until soft and translucent, but not brown.
4. Add the chicken with the marinade, bring to a boil, reduce heat and cook uncovered for about 10 minutes, stirring every so often.
5. Add remaining ingredients (except the coconut milk), simmer covered for about 30 minutes, or until the chicken is done.
6. Remove the cardamom pods and cinnamon stick. Stir in the coconut milk and continue to simmer for another 5 minutes.

Chicken Meat Loaf
Yield: about 6 servings

This makes a hearty dish but nevertheless should be eaten in restricted quantities.

3 shallots (about 4 ounces)
1 medium zucchini (about 5 ounces)
4 cloves garlic
2 eggs, omega-3
1 tablespoon Italian seasoning
4 tablespoons ketchup
1 tablespoon olive oil
4 tablespoons chopped fresh parsley
1 teaspoon salt, or to taste
freshly ground black pepper, to taste
1 pound ground chicken breast, skinless and fatless
1/2 cup (about 2 ounces) almond flour
1 tablespoon coconut flour
olive oil spray

1. Quarter the shallots and roughly slice the zucchini and garlic gloves and combine in your food processor. Using the blade, mix to obtain a finely chopped consistency.
2. Beat the eggs with an electric hand mixer in a large mixing bowl. Mix in the Italian seasoning, ketchup and olive oil. Add the parsley and salt and pepper to taste.
3. Add the ground chicken, and using a fork, combine with the egg mixture.
4. Mix in the almond flour and coconut flour and coat the meat equally (the best way is to use your hands).
5. Spray a loaf mold (9 inches long, 5 inches wide, 3 inches high) with olive oil and fill with the mixture.
6. Bake in a hot oven at 340°F (170°C) for approximately 1 hour. Check for doneness.

Poultry, Game & Meat
Chicken Pot-au-Feu
Yield: 4 servings

A hearty and complete meal in itself. Rich in both vegetables and some chicken, this can be eaten to satiety.

1 pound frozen cauliflower florets
about 2 1/2 cups frozen chopped spinach (about 10 ounces)
1 tablespoon olive oil
1 white onion (about 6 ounces), sliced
3 large cloves garlic, thinly sliced
2 teaspoons stir-fry spices
28-ounce can chopped tomatoes
1 cup vegetable broth, or vegetable juice
2 tablespoons tomato paste
1/2 teaspoon chili sauce (e.g. Sambal Oelek)
salt to taste
freshly ground black pepper, to taste
1 pound zucchini, unpeeled, cut into 1/2-inch slices
about 3/4 pound chicken breast, skinless, cut into bite-size cubes
2 tablespoons chopped fresh parsley

1. Defrost the cauliflower florets and the spinach, following the instructions on the packet. Set aside.
2. Meanwhile heat the olive oil in a large sauce pan and sauté the onion, until soft and translucent, but not brown.
3. Add the garlic slices and stir-fry spices and sauté for 2 more minutes.
4. Add the tomatoes, the vegetable broth, the tomato paste, the chili sauce and salt and pepper to taste. Bring slowly to a boil.
5. Add the zucchini and cook slowly, covered, until almost done, but still crunchy.
6. Add the cauliflower florets and spinach to the saucepan. Adjust the seasoning. Bring to a boil.
7. Reduce heat and add the chicken cubes to the pot, pressing them gently into the mixture with the back of a spoon. Simmer covered all together for about 10 minutes. Check the chicken for doneness.
8. Serve in big individual plates. Prior to serving, sprinkle with the parsley.

Poultry, Game & Meat
Chicken with Cauliflower and Prunes
Yield: up to 4 servings

Moroccans cook many of their dishes in a clay 'tajine' pot where the ingredients slowly bake, covered, and simmering in their own juices. Prunes too are typical of Moroccan cuisine. Here I personally used a Pyrex casserole dish fitted with a domed lid. Since you may not have this kind of lid, I suggested, in the recipe below, to cover the dish with foil.

1 pound chicken breasts, skinless, cut in half
6 tablespoons olive oil
2 teaspoons lemon juice
2 teaspoons lemon peel
salt to taste
black pepper to taste
1 1/2 tablespoons finely chopped shallot
1 1/2 tablespoons dried thyme
1 1/2 pounds cauliflower, cut into florets
10 pitted prunes
6 cloves garlic, sliced
olive oil spray

1. Rinse chicken breasts and pat dry with kitchen paper.
2. Whisk the oil, lemon juice and lemon peel in a small mixing bowl. Salt and pepper to taste. Mix in the chopped shallot. Set aside.
3. Spread out the thyme evenly on the bottom of a medium-size baking dish (say 9x12 inches, or 10x10 inches) and lay out the chicken on top.
4. Brush 2 teaspoons of the oil and lemon mixture over the top of the chicken breasts.
5. Arrange the cauliflower florets, prunes and garlic evenly around the chicken.
6. Distribute the remaining oil and lemon mixture evenly over the cauliflower florets in the baking dish. Additionally spray the top with olive oil.
7. Cover and marinate for about 1 hour in your fridge (or alternatively prepare the day before).
8. Prior to baking, cover with foil. Bake in a hot oven at 340°F (170°C) for about 45 minutes. Uncover and bake for another 15 minutes. Check the chicken and cauliflower for doneness.

Poultry, Game & Meat
Chili Con Carne
Yield: 6 servings

Chili con carne is usually made with beef, but here we substitute chicken. Alternatively you can use any other conforming meat, such as turkey, venison, and so on. Also in our recipe here, we substitute beans by eggplant.

The chili is much tastier a day or two after it's cooked, as the flavors develop and the texture becomes richer.

olive oil spray
2 onions (about 9 ounces), thinly sliced
3 cloves garlic, crushed
1 small carrot (about 3 ounces), peeled and sliced
2 medium celery stalks (about 4 ounces), sliced
2 teaspoons dried chili flakes, or to taste
1 teaspoon ground cumin
1 teaspoon ground coriander
1 tablespoon cinnamon bark pieces
3 tablespoons tomato paste
1 good shake of Worcestershire sauce, to taste
2-3 medium eggplants (around 1 1/4 pound), unpeeled and cut into bite-size pieces
14-ounce can chopped tomatoes
1 cup red wine
salt to taste
freshly ground black pepper, to taste
1 1/4 pound ground chicken breast, skinless and fatless
optional: 3 tablespoons chopped fresh cilantro leaves

1. Spray a large saucepan with the olive oil and sauté the onion until soft and translucent, but not brown.
2. Mix in the garlic, carrot and celery and sauté for another 2 minutes.
3. Add the chili flakes to taste, the cumin, coriander, cinnamon barks and coat the veggies with the spices. Mix in the tomato paste and Worcestershire sauce to taste. Heat through for 2 minutes.
4. Add the eggplant slices and sauté uncovered for about 5 minutes.

5. Mix in the chopped tomatoes with their juice and the red wine.

6. Season with salt and pepper to taste.

7. Bring to a boil, reduce heat and simmer covered for around 20 minutes, or until the eggplant is done.

8. Blend the meat into the eggplant mixture (using a fork to shred during the cooking process). If necessary, adjust the seasoning.

9. Optional: add the chopped cilantro and simmer all together for 2 minutes.

Poultry, Game & Meat
Curry Stir-fry Chicken Breast
Yield: up to 6 servings

A good, conforming, self-contained meal with protein and plant food in good balance. The mild curry spice should just be enough to make the dish piquant (hot, pungent curries are to be avoided).

1 tablespoon olive oil
about 1 1/4 pound chicken breast, skinless, cut into bite-size cubes
salt, to taste
freshly ground black pepper, to taste
2 tablespoons cumin seeds
2 onions (about 3/4 pound), thinly sliced
4 gloves garlic, crushed
3-4 tablespoons mild curry paste, to taste
2 green bell peppers (about 14 ounces), seeded and sliced
2 red bell peppers (about 14 ounces), seeded and sliced
28-ounce can chopped tomatoes

1. Heat the oil in a large, non-stick frying pan (or wok). Add the chicken and sauté for a few minutes until golden brown on both sides. Salt and pepper to taste. Set aside on a hot plate and cover.
2. Add the cumin seeds to the frying pan and stir-fry for 2 minutes. Add the onion and sauté, until soft and translucent, but not brown. Stir in the garlic and curry paste to taste.
3. Add the green bell peppers and sauté until they soften (green bell peppers take longer to cook than red ones).
4. Mix in the red bell peppers and stir-fry for another 5 minutes.
5. Add the chopped tomatoes. Salt and pepper to taste. Bring slowly to a boil. Reduce heat, cover and simmer for about 10 minutes.
6. Add the chicken cubes, pressing them gently into the mixture with the back of a spoon.
7. Simmer for about 5 minutes. Check chicken and vegetables for doneness.

Poultry, Game & Meat
Dr Rita's Chicken Marsala
Yield: up to 4 servings

During one of Geoff's California lecture tours, Dr Rita Stec (Author of 'A Woman's Home Health Companion') kindly invited us to dinner. She has been a faithful supporter of Geoff's work for many years, and she served up this dish which we found excellent.

1 pound organic, free range, skinless chicken breast
olive oil spray
2 cups (about 4 ounces) sliced fresh mushrooms
1 tablespoon Italian seasoning
garlic salt, to taste
1 cup Marsala wine
1/2 – 1 cup (about 3-6 ounces) 'Mock Mashed Potato Purée' (see recipe page 92), more or less, as required for thickening

1. Pound chicken breasts to 1/4-inch thick and cut into bite-size cubes.
2. Spray a frying pan with the olive oil and sauté the chicken briefly, until golden brown. Set aside on a plate and cover with foil.
3. Now sauté the mushrooms in the same pan on medium-high heat, stirring constantly all the time, until they release their juices. Season with Italian seasoning and garlic salt to taste.
4. Add chicken and Marsala wine to mushrooms in pan and simmer on low heat, covered, until chicken is cooked through.
5. Stir in the 'Mock Mashed Potato Purée', enough to thicken the sauce.
6. Serve either alone or over 'Mock Mashed Potato Purée'.

Poultry, Game & Meat
Duck Breast in Red Wine
Yield: 4 servings

Duck breast, without the skin and fat, is very close to the kind of fowl, eaten by our Pleistocene ancestors. Because of its low fat content, expect it to be drier and more chewy than farm-bred poultry. Serve with 'Mock Mashed Potato Purée' (see recipe page 92) as a side dish.

olive oil spray
2 tablespoons thinly chopped shallots
1 cup red wine
1 bay leaf
1 cup chicken broth
2 cloves garlic, crushed
salt to taste
freshly ground black pepper, to taste
2 duck breasts, skin and fat removed (about 5-6 ounces **each**)

1. Spray a medium-size, non-stick frying pan with the olive oil and sauté the shallots on medium heat, until soft and translucent, but not brown.
2. Add the wine and the bay leaf. Bring to a boil. Reduce heat and simmer uncovered for about 8-10 minutes, until the liquid has reduced to about 1/2 cup.
3. Strain through a sieve. Pour the sauce into a medium-size saucepan. Add the chicken broth and the garlic. Bring to a boil. Season with salt and pepper to taste. Cover the broth and keep the sauce pan heated on the stove.
4. Sauté the duck breasts in a medium-size, non-stick frying pan (no oil added) on medium-high heat for about 2 minutes on each side. The duck meat should still be pink inside. Salt and pepper to taste.
5. Place the duck breasts into the hot broth in the saucepan. Cover and remove from stove. Allow the meat to soak for approximately 10 minutes.
6. Prior to serving, remove the duck breast from the broth and cut into thick slices. Serve on a hot serving plate, or 4 individual plates, topped with a little sauce. The rest of the sauce should be served separately.

Poultry, Game & Meat
Hunter's Stew
Yield: 8 servings

This recipe is a classic way of preparing hunted meats. It uses the technique (marinating) of soaking the meat in a flavorful liquid to tenderize the meat and enrich its flavor. Here we use goat, but you can try this recipe on other game meat too, e.g. venison, wild boar, elk etc.

Marinade:
1/2 bottle cheap dry red wine
1 onion (about 4 ounces), sliced
3 garlic cloves, sliced
1 teaspoon peppercorns
1 tablespoon cinnamon bark pieces
3 bay leaves
3 sprigs fresh oregano or thyme
(or 2 teaspoons dried herbs)
Stew:
2 pounds goat meat, cut into 1-inch cubes
2 tablespoons olive oil
about 1 pound onions, sliced
5 gloves garlic, crushed
2 tablespoons tomato paste
about 1 pound green bell peppers, seeded and sliced
about 2 pounds zucchini, sliced
1/2 white cabbage (about 1 pound), sliced
salt to taste
freshly ground black pepper, to taste
2 teaspoons Italian seasoning
1 teaspoon ground coriander
1 teaspoon ground cumin
Tabasco sauce to taste

1. Prepare the marinade in a medium-size dish. Leave the meat to marinate, covered with a lid or foil, for up to 4 days in the fridge (the meat should be covered by the marinade – if not, turn the meat from time to time).
2. On the day you cook it: drain the goat meat in a colander, but collect the liquid and keep the onion and garlic apart. Set aside.

3. Heat 1 tablespoon of the oil in a large sauce pan. Add the drained goat meat and sauté until golden brown on both sides. Set aside on a plate and cover.

4. Add the remaining tablespoon of oil to the pan and sauté the onion until it is soft and translucent, but not brown.

5. Add the garlic and sauté for 2 minutes.

6. Mix in the tomato paste and coat the onion.

7. Add the left-over marinated onion and garlic, together with the green bell peppers. Sauté for 5 minutes.

8. Mix in the zucchini and the cabbage.

9. Season with salt and pepper to taste. Add the Italian seasoning, the coriander, the cumin and the Tabasco sauce to taste.

10. Add the marinade liquid, as needed, to moisten the vegetables.

11. Cook covered, until the veggies are half-way cooked, but still very crunchy.

12. Add the goat meat. Simmer all together for about 15 minutes, or more if needed. Check the meat for doneness.

Poultry, Game & Meat
Moroccan Chicken
Yield: up to 6 servings

A colorful dish full of exotic flavors, typical of Moroccan cuisine.

Serve with simply cooked vegetables, such as green beans etc.

3 tablespoons olive oil
3 tablespoons freshly squeezed lemon juice, or to taste
2 teaspoons ground cumin
2 teaspoons ground cinnamon
2 chili peppers, seeded and finely chopped
3 cloves garlic, crushed
4 tablespoons raisins
4 tablespoons pine nuts
1/2 teaspoon salt, or to taste
4 tablespoons finely chopped fresh mint
about 1 1/4 pounds chicken breast, skinless, cut into bite-size cubes

1. Mix olive oil and lemon juice in a medium-size mixing bowl with a fork. Mix in the cumin, cinnamon, chili peppers and garlic. Add the raisins and pine nuts. Season with salt to taste. Add 3 tablespoons of the chopped mint.
2. Add the chicken to the mixture and coat well with the ingredients. Cover the dish and place in your fridge for 1/2 hour.
3. Heat a frying pan to medium-high heat. Add the chicken with its mixture and sauté on both sides, until golden brown.
4. Reduce heat, cover and simmer on low heat until the chicken is fully cooked (about 5 minutes). Check for doneness.
5. Prior to serving, mix in the remaining tablespoon of mint.

Poultry, Game & Meat
Paleo Moussaka
Yield: 6 servings

This typical Greek dish is usually made with lamb. All we need to do is substitute the meat with a better fatty acid profile meat, such as chicken (or you can use any other fowl or wild game). Cheese is not part of the traditional Mediterranean dish, but has become common in Western cooking. Not for the purist!

3 pounds eggplant, sliced lengthways into 1/4-inch thick slices
2 tablespoons olive oil
1 1/4 pounds ground chicken breast, skinless and fatless
salt to taste
freshly ground black pepper, to taste
2 jars ready-made marinara sauce (14 ounces **each**)
Tabasco sauce, to taste
olive oil spray
optional: 1/2 cup (about 2 ounces) grated Parmesan, or Mozzarella cheese – the purist will leave it out

1. Steam the eggplant slices for 10-15 minutes or until cooked. Separate them into three lots. Set aside.
2. Heat the oil in a big, nonstick frying pan and sauté the ground chicken, taking care to separate it (using a fork to shred) during the cooking process. The chicken meat should be golden brown. Salt and pepper to taste.
3. Add the marinara sauce to the chicken and heat through all together. Season with the Tabasco sauce to taste.
4. Spray a large-size (and preferably square), table-ready baking dish with olive oil. Cover the bottom with the first lot of the eggplant slices. Salt and pepper to taste.
5. Take half of the chicken and marinara mixture and spread it over the first eggplant layer. Place the second lot of eggplant in the next layer. Salt and pepper to taste.
6. Spread the remaining chicken and marinara mixture over the eggplant slices. Place the third lot of eggplant slices in a final layer to cover the whole dish. Salt and pepper to taste.
7. Sprinkle with Parmesan, or Mozzarella cheese (optional – the health purist will leave it out).
8. Heat through in a hot oven at 340°F (170°C) for about 10-15 minutes, or until the cheese is melted.

Poultry, Game & Meat
Quince and Chicken Curry
Yield: up to 6 servings

Quince is a good fruit, low glycemic and rich in the usual assortment of micro-nutrients. It is also rich in pectin – a gum like plant fiber – which makes quince a suitable ingredient for dishes which have to 'set', like jams and jellies. This property helps thicken the sauce.

Quince contributes a pleasant, distinctive aroma to the dish. Raw quince has a strongly tart and astringent taste, which is removed by the cooking and tasty spices.

1 tablespoon olive oil
about 1 1/4 pounds skinless chicken breast, cut into bite-size cubes
salt to taste
ground black pepper, to taste
about 1/2 pound sugar snaps
about 1 1/2 pounds quince
2 tablespoons grated ginger
3 gloves garlic, chopped
3 tablespoons mild curry paste, to taste
about 1/2 pound carrots, peeled and cut into thick slices
1 1/4 cups coconut milk
3/4 cup vegetable broth
2 tablespoons light soy sauce, or to taste
1 teaspoon sesame oil
3 green onions, sliced
2 tablespoons chopped fresh cilantro leaves

1. Heat the oil in a large sauce pan. Add the chicken and sauté until golden brown on both sides. Salt and pepper to taste. Set aside on a hot plate and cover.
2. Meanwhile blanch the sugar snaps in boiling water for 2 minutes. Drain and set aside.
3. Peel the quince, quarter and core it (there will be some waste). Cut out any woody parts. Cut into thick slices and set aside.
4. Add the ginger and garlic to the sauce pan and stir-fry for 2 minutes. Mix in the curry paste and the carrot slices and sauté all together for another 2 minutes.

5. Add the quince, the coconut milk and vegetable broth. Bring slowly to a boil, cover and simmer for 10-15 minutes, or until the vegetables are cooked.

6. Season with the soy sauce and sesame oil.

7. Add the chicken, sugar snaps and green onions to the curry. Simmer all together for about 5 minutes. Check the chicken for doneness.

8. Prior to serving, mix in the cilantro leaves.

Spicy Chicken in Coconut
Yield: 6 servings

This interesting combination of eastern spices makes for a flavorful, slightly piquant dish that is always popular.

1 tablespoon olive oil
about 1 1/2 pounds skinless chicken breast, cut into bit-size cubes
2 medium white onions (about 3/4 pound), thinly sliced
2 teaspoons grated ginger
8 medium cloves garlic, sliced
1/2 cup water
12 bay leaves
1 pound fresh tomatoes, chopped
1 cup coconut milk
1/4 – 1/2 cup water, as needed
Spice blend:
1 tablespoon poppy seeds
1 heaped tablespoon coriander seeds
1 1/2 teaspoons cumin seeds
1/2 teaspoon turmeric
1 teaspoon Garam Masala
1/2 – 1 teaspoon red chili flakes, to taste

1. Heat the oil in a large frying pan (or wok). Add the chicken and sauté until golden brown on both sides. Set aside on a hot plate and cover.
2. Sauté the onion in the same pan, until soft and translucent, but not brown.
3. Meanwhile, using a blender, mix the ginger, garlic and water, until you obtain a fine paste. Add to the onion in the pan.
4. Mix also the spice blend into the onion. Add the bay leaves.
5. Return the chicken to the pan. Make sure that the meat is well coated with onion and spices. Stir-fry for a few minutes.
6. Mix in the chopped tomatoes. Bring slowly to a boil. Reduce heat and simmer covered for about 10 minutes.
7. Mix in the coconut milk and water (more or less, as needed for thickness). Simmer uncovered, for about 5 minutes. Check the chicken for doneness.

Poultry, Game & Meat
Venison Burgers
Yield: up to 6 servings

This makes a hearty and tasty burger. The venison is a safe meat that, like all high protein foods, should nevertheless be eaten in restricted quantities.

1 1/4 pounds ground venison burger meat
2 shallots (about 3 ounces)
3 cloves garlic
5 sprigs fresh parsley
2 eggs, omega-3
2 tablespoons coconut flour
1 teaspoon paprika powder
1 teaspoon Worcester sauce
1/2 teaspoon salt, or to taste
freshly ground black pepper, to taste
olive oil spray

1. Place the burger meat in a large bowl. Set aside.
2. Combine shallots, garlic and parsley in a food processor and, using the blade, blend to a finely chopped consistency. Add to the burger meat in the bowl.
3. Beat the eggs with an electric hand-mixer in a medium-size mixing bowl. Blend in the coconut flour, paprika and Worcester sauce. Salt and pepper to taste.
4. Add the egg mixture to the venison meat. Using a fork (or better, use your hands) coat the burger meat uniformly with the egg mixture.
5. Form patties with your hands, any size you wish to give them.
6. Spray a large, non-stick frying pan with the oil and sauté the burgers from both sides, until golden brown. Then cover and fry until the center is cooked.

Poultry, Game & Meat
Venison Steak
Yield: 4 servings

We suggest serving the venison steaks and sauce together with 'Mock Mashed Potato Purée' (see recipe page 92). It makes a fine centerpiece for a festive dinner.

Marinade:
red wine (enough to cover the venison)
1 red onion (about 4 ounces), sliced
2 cloves garlic, crushed
1/2 teaspoon grated ginger
1 bay leaf
1 teaspoon grated orange peel

about 1 pound wild venison, fresh or frozen
2 tablespoons freshly squeezed orange juice
olive oil spray
salt to taste
freshly ground black pepper, to taste

1. Combine the marinade ingredients in a medium-size dish and leave the meat to marinate for 24 hours (whether the venison is fresh or frozen). There should be enough marinade to cover the meat – if not, turn the meat from time to time. Cover the dish with a lid or foil.
2. The following day, take out the meat, but collect the liquid. Strain the marinade through a fine sieve and pour into a small saucepan. Add the orange juice and bring to a boil. Reduce to half of the original volume. Set aside.
3. Pat dry the venison meat with kitchen paper and cut into 4 steaks. Spray both sides of the meat with olive oil and salt and pepper to taste.
4. Spray a non-stick frying pan with the oil and sauté the steaks on medium-high heat for a few minutes on each side.
5. Add a little amount of the sauce to the steaks. Cover and simmer on low heat for about 5 minutes, or until the meat is cooked, but still lightly pink inside.
6. Serve the sauce on the side

.

CHAPTER 7
Seafood

Avocado and Crab Cakes
Yield: 10 muffin-size (2.5-inch diameter) crab-cakes

These healthy mini 'cakes' make a tasty starter or party snack.

2 cans crab meat (6 ounces net weight **each**)
2 ripe avocados (each about 7 ounces), stoned and peeled
2 tablespoons lime juice
5 drops Tabasco sauce, or to taste
salt taste
freshly ground black pepper, to taste
4 small gelatin sheets*
1 tablespoon finely chopped parsley

1. Drain the crabmeat thoroughly (and set aside in a medium size mixing bowl), but collect the liquid into a measuring cup. The liquid will amount to about 3/4 cup. Set aside.
2. Mix the avocado flesh in your blender or food-processor, together with the lime juice. Season with Tabasco, salt and pepper to taste. Transfer to the mixing bowl with the crabmeat and combine carefully with a fork.
3. Meanwhile soak the gelatin sheets in a bowl of cold water for 10 minutes.
4. Heat the crab juice in a small saucepan and bring to a boil. Set aside for 5 minutes.
5. Lift gelatin sheets from the cold water and squeeze gently to remove excess water. Add to the warm crab juice in the saucepan, stirring until dissolved. Add the mixture to the avocado-crab mixture in the mixing bowl. Mix in the chopped parsley and re-adjust the seasoning, if needed.
6. Divide the mixture equally amongst 10 muffin molds. Refrigerate until set (at least 4 hours), or until the next day. Serve de-molded.

* Here I used gelatin sheets measuring 4.6 x 2.75 inches. They can be replaced by agar-agar which is a seaweed extract and is used as a vegan thickener and can be found in every Health Food Store and online.

Seafood
Cod Fish Loaf
Yield: about 6 servings

A good, conforming, high protein dish, to serve as part of a main meal. Also much appreciated when served cold at party buffets.

olive oil spray
5 cloves garlic, crushed
28-ounce can chopped tomatoes
salt to taste
freshly ground black pepper, to taste
1 1/2 pounds cod fillets
6 eggs, omega-3
1 pinch cayenne pepper, or to taste
4 tablespoons chopped fresh basil

1. Spray a large frying pan with the olive oil and sauté the garlic rapidly.
2. Add the chopped tomatoes. Salt and pepper to taste. Cook uncovered over medium heat. When most of the liquid has evaporated, reduce the heat. Simmer, uncovered, stirring frequently, until the tomatoes start to stick to the pan (the cooking time may take up to 50 minutes). Set aside.
3. Meanwhile coarsely chop the raw fish fillets by hand. Set aside.
4. Beat the eggs in a large mixing bowl with an electric hand-mixer. Salt and pepper to taste. Add a pinch of cayenne pepper, or more to taste.
5. Add the tomatoes, the fish and the basil to the eggs, and using a fork, mix all together evenly. If necessary, adjust the seasoning.
6. Spray a large round baking mold (9 or 10 inches diameter) with the olive oil and fill with the mixture.
7. Bake in a hot oven at 340°F (170°C) for about 1 hour. Check for doneness.
8. This dish can be served directly in the mold. Or if desired, de-mold before serving, but then allow to cool down first. Best served cold.

Seafood
Crab St. Jacques au Gratin
Yield: 4 servings

Eat as a starter, or as an accompaniment to a big salad. The 'St. Jacques' style normally employs 'bad' ingredients, such as double cream, butter and flour. Here, in this recipe, we achieve a dish with all the same flavor and delicious taste, but without the bad ingredients.

2 cans crab meat (6 ounces net weight **each**)
2/3 cup clam juice (more or less as needed)
1 pound 'Mock Mashed Potato Purée' (see page 92), more or less, as needed for required thickness
2 pinches nutmeg
salt taste
freshly ground black pepper, to taste
olive oil spray
optional: 1/2 cup grated Swiss cheese (about 2 ounces) - the purist will leave it out

1. Drain the crabmeat thoroughly (and set aside), but collect the liquid into a measuring cup. The liquid will amount to about 2/3 cup.
2. In a bowl mix the crab liquid with the clam juice.
3. Add the 'Mock Mashed Potato Purée' and blend slowly into the liquid with a whisk, until you obtain a smooth consistency.
4. Stir in the crabmeat.
5. Season with the nutmeg, salt and pepper to taste.
6. Spray 4 individual small, ovenproof molds with the olive oil and fill with the mixture.
7. Optional: sprinkle the cheese over the top of the dishes (the purist will leave it out).
8. Brown under the grill, until the surface has a golden color (take care to keep the dish at a certain distance from the grill).
9. Serve the molds directly to the table.

Seafood
Grilled Ahi Tuna
Yield: 2 servings

This is a fine omega-3 rich meal. The same recipe can be used for other types of fish too, such as shark and salmon.

Sauce:
2 teaspoons Dijon mustard
2 tablespoons olive oil
1 tablespoon fresh lemon juice
1/4 teaspoon salt
freshly ground black pepper, to taste
2-3 shallots (about 2 ounces), finely chopped

2 Ahi Tuna steaks (about 4-5 ounces **each**)
olive oil spray

1. Combine the ingredients for the sauce (except the shallots) in a small bowl and blend with a hand whisk, until you obtain a creamy sauce. Mix in the shallots.
2. Coat the tuna steaks from both sides with the mixture. Set aside the rest of the sauce.
3. Spray a small baking dish with the olive oil and lay out the fish on the bottom.
4. Pour the rest of the sauce over the fish.
5. Grill the fish for about 5 minutes, or depending on how rare you like it.

Seafood
Prawn Tails in Coconut Sauce
Yield: 2 servings

A nice balance of Asian flavors and nutrients.
Serving suggestion: 'Cauliflower Risotto' (see page 84) or 'Mock Mashed Potato Purée' (see page 92).

1/2 pound frozen prawn tails
1-2 tablespoons lemon juice, to taste
olive oil spray
1 white onion (about 5 ounces), finely chopped
1 clove garlic, crushed
1 teaspoon grated fresh ginger
1 1/2 teaspoons mild curry powder, or to taste
2 medium tomatoes (about 10 ounces)
salt, to taste
ground black pepper, to taste
1/2 cup coconut milk
2 tablespoons chopped fresh parsley

1. Defrost the prawns and rinse them briefly.
2. Marinate for 30 minutes in the lemon juice. Drain the prawns and pat dry with kitchen paper.
3. Spray a large, non-stick frying pan with the oil and sauté the prawns briefly on both sides for only a few minutes, until golden brown. Set aside on a hot plate.
4. Sauté the onions in the same frying pan until soft and translucent, but not brown.
5. Mix in the garlic, ginger and curry powder to taste and sauté for a few minutes.
6. Meanwhile quarter the tomatoes, seed and chop them. Add to the onions in the pan and salt and pepper to taste. Cover and simmer for 3-5 minutes. The tomatoes should still stay crunchy.
7. Stir in the coconut milk and heat through.
8. Return the prawns to the pan and mix in the parsley. Heat through all together for a further 2 minutes.

Seafood
Red Snapper Casablanca
Yield: 4 servings

The subtle, spicy tang of Arabia brings an exotic flavor to this perfect preparation of Red Snapper. It is a good dish for a buffet.

olive oil spray
4 red snapper fillets (about 1 pound)
salt to taste
freshly ground black pepper, to taste
1 white onion (about 4-5 ounces), finely chopped
1 large red bell pepper (about 1/2 pound), seeded and finely chopped
2 cloves garlic, crushed
1 pinch red chili powder, or to taste
1/2 teaspoon thyme, fresh or dried
2 tablespoons chopped fresh mint
2 tablespoons fresh lemon juice
1 tablespoon white wine

1. Spray a non-stick frying pan with the olive oil and sauté rapidly the fish fillets from both sides for about 2 minutes, or until done and golden brown. Salt and pepper to taste. Set aside on a serving dish.
2. Spray some more olive oil in the frying pan and sauté the onion, bell pepper and garlic, until tender and soft.
3. Season with the chili powder to taste. Mix in the thyme, 1 tablespoon of the mint, the lemon juice and white wine.
4. Simmer all together for 2 minutes. Salt lightly and pepper to taste.
5. Layer the vegetable mixture over the fish fillets on the serving dish.
6. Sprinkle with the remaining tablespoon of mint.
7. This dish can be served, either hot or cold.

Seafood
Salmon Loaf Quick-Fix
Yield: up to 6 servings

This dish is good for buffets and cocktail snacks, as well as normal meals.

7-8 ounces canned salmon (or the left-over of cooked salmon)
olive oil spray
2 cloves garlic, crushed (or 2 teaspoons ready-made garlic paste)
14-ounce can chopped tomatoes
freshly ground black pepper, to taste
salt to taste
4 eggs, omega-3
2 tablespoons chopped fresh parsley

1. Clean the salmon from its skin and backbone (if any) and break it up with a fork. Set aside.
2. Spray a large frying pan with the olive oil and sauté the garlic briefly.
3. Add the tomatoes and cook uncovered over medium heat, until the tomatoes start to stick to the pan and all the liquid has evaporated. Pepper to taste, salt sparingly (or not at all) since canned salmon is already salty. Set aside.
4. Meanwhile beat the eggs in a medium-size mixing bowl with a hand whisk. Salt and pepper lightly.
5. Incorporate, using a fork, the tomatoes, the fish and the parsley and coat with the eggs.
6. Spray a loaf mold (say, 9 inches long, 4 inches wide and 3 inches high) with the olive oil and fill with the mixture.
7. Bake in a hot oven at 340°F (170°C) for about 35 minutes. Check for doneness.
8. Serve directly in the mold, or allow to cool and then de-mold.

Seafood
Salmon Steaks with Capers
Yield: 2 servings

This is the classic baked salmon, rich in fish oils, but spiced up with the addition of interesting flavors from the capers and French mustard.

2 salmon steaks (about 5-6 ounces **each**)
olive oil spray
2 teaspoons Dijon mustard
1 tablespoon olive oil
2 cloves garlic, crushed
2 tablespoons slivered almonds
1 tablespoon capers, drained

1. Rinse the salmon steaks under running water. Drain and pat dry with kitchen paper.
2. Spray a medium-size baking dish with the oil and lay out the salmon steaks on the bottom, skin-side down.
3. Combine the mustard, olive oil and garlic in a small mixing bowl. Coat the top side of the steaks with the mixture.
4. Bake the salmon in a hot oven at 340°F (170°C) for about 12-15 minutes. Check for doneness.
5. Meanwhile spray a small frying pan with the oil and sauté briefly the slivered almonds. Mix in the capers and heat through.
6. Cover the top of the steaks with a layer of the almond-caper mixture and serve immediately.

Seafood
Samia's Sassy Salmon Patties
Yield: 8 patties (2.5-inch diameter)

Created by Samia, a skillful cook and longtime follower from the United States, this recipe makes a delicious, fully conforming fish cake.

1 can (about 14 ounces) wild caught Alaskan Salmon
1 onion (about 4 ounces)
1/2 medium red bell pepper (about 2 ounces)
1/2 medium green bell pepper (about 2 ounces)
1 celery stalk (about 1 ounce)
5 garlic cloves
7 or 8 sprigs parsley
olive oil spray
2 eggs, omega-3
1 tablespoon olive oil
1 tablespoon Dijon mustard
ground black pepper, to taste
2 tablespoons flax seed flour
optional: fresh lemon juice

1. Drain the liquid and clean the salmon from its skin and backbone (if any). Break it up with a fork and place it in a medium-size mixing bowl. Set aside.
2. Cut roughly the onion, red and green bell pepper, celery stalk and garlic cloves. Combine, together with the parsley, in a food processor and using the blade, mix to obtain a finely chopped consistency.
3. Spray a frying pan with the olive oil and sauté the veggie mixture for about 5 minutes, stirring often. Transfer the veggies to the bowl with the salmon and blend all together, using a fork.
4. Meanwhile beat the eggs with a hand whisk in a small mixing bowl. Add the oil, mustard and pepper to taste. Blend in the flax seed flour.
5. Add the egg mixture to the salmon-vegetable mixture. Blend all together, using a fork or spatula.
6. Line a baking tray with non-stick baking paper and spoon out the salmon mixture onto it. Flatten with a fork and, using a (say)

Seafood

2.5-inch diameter cookie cutter, form into patties. The mixture should yield about 8 patties.

7. Bake with fan heat at 300°F (150°C) for around 25 minutes. Turn over each patty carefully and cook for another 10 minutes, or until golden brown from both sides.

8. Optional: prior to serving sprinkle a few drops of lemon juice on each patty.

Seafood
Sardine Soufflé on Bond Toast
Yield: 4 toasts

An interesting and sophisticated variant on traditional sardines on toast.

1 can (about 4 ounces) sardines in olive oil*
4 slices of conforming Bond bread (see e.g. Three Flour Bread recipe, page 59)
1 egg white, omega-3
ground black pepper, to taste
ground paprika, to taste

1. Drain the sardines and remove the backbones. Crush sardines with a fork. Set aside.
2. Lightly toast (in toaster) 4 slices of bread. Arrange them on the oven grill shelf.
3. Beat the egg white with an electric hand-mixer in a small mixing bowl to a stiff consistency.
4. Mix the egg white carefully into the sardines. Pepper to taste.
5. Spread the sardine mix uniformly on the bread slices, making sure to cover the edges.
6. Grill for around 10 minutes, or until the top is golden brown.
7. Sprinkle with ground paprika to taste and serve immediately.

* The sardines in oil can be replaced by mackerel or sardines in tomato sauce.

Seafood
Spicy Asian Fish
Yield: up to 6 servings

This lightly spiced dish gets its piquant and typical Asian flavor from ginger and lemon grass. Most kinds of thick white fish can be used. This dish can be eaten on its own or served with a green salad.

1 tablespoon olive oil
1 pound onion, sliced
4 large cloves garlic, crushed
2 tablespoons grated fresh ginger
1 tablespoon finely chopped fresh lemon grass
1 teaspoon ground turmeric
2 tablespoons balsamic vinegar
1 tablespoon fish sauce
1 pound tomatoes, seeded and roughly chopped
salt to taste
freshly ground black pepper, to taste
1 1/2 pounds white, boneless fish fillets (catfish, monkfish etc.), cut into 1-inch cubes
2 tablespoons chopped fresh cilantro

1. Heat the olive oil in a large saucepan and sauté the onion, until soft and translucent, but not brown.
2. Stir in the garlic, ginger, lemon grass, turmeric, vinegar and fish sauce and bring slowly to a boil. Reduce heat and simmer, uncovered, for 3 minutes.
3. Stir in the tomatoes and bring slowly to a boil. Salt and pepper to taste.
4. Reduce heat and simmer covered for approximately 10 minutes. The tomatoes should still stay crunchy.
5. Fold the fish into the tomato mixture. Bring slowly to a boil, then immediately reduce heat and simmer, covered, for 5 minutes, or until the fish is tender. Check for doneness.
6. Serve sprinkled with the chopped cilantro.

Seafood
Swordfish on Fennel Bed
Yield: 4 servings

A simply prepared dish. The fennel flavors agreeably complement the chunky swordfish taste. The ratio of vegetables to protein is good at about 3:1 – so it makes a meal in itself.

2 fennel bulbs (about 1 1/4 pounds)
5 tablespoons freshly squeezed orange juice
4-ounce can chopped black olives
olive oil spray
about 1 1/4 pounds Roma tomatoes (or round tomatoes), seeded and coarsely chopped into bite-size chunks
salt to taste
ground black pepper, to taste
1 tablespoon olive oil
2 cloves garlic, crushed
1 1/4 pounds swordfish steaks

1. Trim the green fronds from the fennel bulb and save for garnish. Clean the fennel bulbs, remove the stringy parts (as with celery). Cut each bulb in quarters and slice thinly.
2. Combine the fennel with the orange juice and olives in a large mixing bowl.
3. Spray a large baking dish with the olive oil and spoon the mixture into it.
4. Lay out the tomatoes over the top. Salt and pepper to taste.
5. Cover with aluminum foil and bake in a hot oven at 340°F (170°C) for about 35-40 minutes, stirring once. Check the vegetables for doneness.
6. Meanwhile combine, in a small bowl, the tablespoon of oil with the garlic. Pepper to taste and salt sparingly. Brush the oil mixture evenly over the fish.
7. Place the fish steaks on top of the cooked vegetables in the baking dish, cover with the foil and bake for another 15 minutes, or until the fish is done.

Seafood
Trout Marrakech
Yield: up to 4 servings

This is a real showpiece for a dinner table or a buffet! A whole fish prepared in the Moroccan style! It uses the exotic spices of Morocco and you can be sure to impress your guests.

Fish:
1 trout (about 1 pound), cleaned
salt to taste
freshly ground black pepper, to taste
olive oil spray
1 red onion (about 5 ounces), thinly sliced
4 tablespoons white wine
2 pinches saffron

Stuffing:
2 tablespoons olive oil
1 tablespoon water
1 1/2 tablespoons xylitol
1 teaspoon ground cinnamon
2 teaspoons orange blossom water (optional)
salt (moderate)
freshly ground black pepper, to taste
1/2 cup almond flakes (about 2 ounces)

1. **Fish**: season the trout on the inside with salt (moderate) and pepper. Set aside.
2. Spray a large baking dish with the olive oil and lay out the onion on the bottom of the dish.
3. Combine the white wine with the saffron in a small mixing bowl. Pour the wine equally over the onion in the dish.
4. **Stuffing**: in a medium-size mixing bowl whisk all the stuffing ingredients with a fork, except the almond flakes, which you blend in last.
5. Place half of the stuffing inside the trout.
6. Lay the fish on top of the onion in the baking dish. Spread the remaining stuffing over the top of the fish.
7. Bake in a hot oven at 340°F (170°C) for approximately 35-40 minutes. Check the fish for doneness.

Seafood
Tuna and Tomato Bake
Yield: 2 servings

The tuna steak is buried in a deep pile of flavorful tomatoes and onion.

There is a good ratio of protein to plant food – about 1 to 4 – and what ingredients! Good, healthy tuna, and the tomato and onion full of essential flavonoids.

2 pounds fresh tomatoes (or a 28-ounce can chopped tomatoes)
1 tuna steak (about 10 ounces)
4 cloves garlic, crushed
1 teaspoon paprika powder
2 teaspoons Italian seasoning
salt to taste
freshly ground black pepper, to taste
olive oil spray
2 white onions (about 1/2 pound), thinly sliced
a few drops of Tabasco Sauce, to taste
1 tablespoon chopped fresh basil

1. Place the tomatoes in a large bowl and pour boiling water over them. Set aside for 1 minute. Drain the tomatoes, peel off the skin and cut into 1/2-inch thick slices. Set aside in a colander (if you use canned tomatoes, drain their liquid first).
2. Coat the tuna on both sides with 2 crushed garlic cloves, the paprika and 1 teaspoon of the Italian seasoning. Dust lightly with salt and pepper to taste. Set aside (to make it even tastier, you can prepare the tuna in advance and marinate in your fridge).
3. Spray a medium-size baking dish with the oil and spread out the onion. Coat the onion with another spray of olive oil.
4. Place the tomatoes on top. Distribute the remaining garlic equally amongst the tomatoes. Salt and pepper to taste and season with the remaining Italian seasoning and Tabasco sauce to taste.
5. Bake in a hot oven at 340°F (170°C) for about 25 minutes.
6. Now dig a hole in the middle of the veggies and place the tuna into it. Cover with the veggies and bake for another 15-20 minutes, or until the fish is cooked.
7. Prior to serving, sprinkle with the chopped basil.

Seafood
Tuna and Zucchini Gratin
Yield: 6 servings

The challenge of making zucchini into a flavorful dish is successfully achieved by the judicious choice of spices. Overall, the dish achieves a good balance of plant food and protein.

olive oil spray
1/2 pound red onion, thinly sliced
4 cloves garlic, crushed
1/2 teaspoon hot chili sauce, or to taste
2 pounds zucchini, unpeeled and thinly sliced
3 teaspoons Italian seasoning
salt to taste
freshly ground black pepper to taste
1 teaspoon lemon juice
6 eggs, omega-3
2 cans tuna flakes (4.5 ounces **each**), drained

1. Spray a large frying pan with the oil and sauté the onion, until soft and translucent, but not brown.
2. Mix in the garlic, the chili sauce to taste and sauté all together.
3. Add the zucchini, sprinkle with the Italian seasoning and salt and pepper to taste. Coat the zucchini with the ingredients and bring slowly to a boil. Reduce heat and simmer covered for 20 minutes. The veggies should still be crunchy. Mix in the lemon juice. Set aside.
4. Meanwhile beat the eggs with a hand-whisk in a large mixing bowl. Salt and pepper to taste.
5. Add the zucchini mixture and the tuna flakes to the eggs, mixing all together and leaving a coarse texture.
6. Spray a loaf mold (say, 9 inches long, 5 inches wide, 3 inches high) with the olive oil and fill with the mixture.
7. Bake in a hot oven at 340°F (170°C) for about 55 minutes, or until the eggs are done.
8. Serve hot or cold.

Seafood
Wahoo Steak and Vegetables
Yield: 2 servings

Wahoo is a fish related to the tuna and swordfish. They can be used instead, if you cannot find Wahoo. This is a quick and healthy dish. To maintain a good protein/plant balance, you should serve the dish with extra vegetables, such as steamed green beans for example.

1 Wahoo steak (about 10 ounces), frozen or fresh
1 tablespoon fresh lemon juice
olive oil spray
1 1/2 cups sliced mushrooms (about 3 ounces)
4 green onions, sliced
1 tablespoon white wine
2 teaspoons Italian seasoning
salt to taste
freshly ground black pepper, to taste
1/2 teaspoon curry powder, or to taste
2 medium zucchini (about 3/4 pound), sliced
optional: 2 medium tomatoes (about 1/2 pound), seeded and sliced

1. Rinse the steak and pat it dry (if frozen, no need to defrost). Sprinkle both sides with the lemon juice and set aside to marinate.
2. Spray a microwave-proof baking dish with the olive oil and distribute the mushrooms and green onions on the bottom.
3. Drizzle the white wine and sprinkle half of the Italian seasoning over the top. Salt (sparingly) and pepper to taste.
4. Pat dry a second time the Wahoo steak. Spray both sides with olive oil and sprinkle with the curry powder. Place the fish on top of the mushroom and onion mixture in the dish.
5. Lay out the zucchini slices over the fish steak and sprinkle with the rest of the Italian seasoning. Salt and pepper to taste. Spray a little olive oil over the top. Optional: place the tomatoes on top of the zucchini and adjust the seasoning.
6. Cover and cook in the microwave on high power (or 650 Watt) for about 10 minutes. Check the fish and vegetables for doneness.

CHAPTER 8
Desserts

Aniseed Spice Cake
Yield: up to 16 squares

This makes a delicious, conforming cake that can be eaten at any time of day. For example, for a quick continental breakfast or at afternoon tea.

5 tablespoons aniseeds
5 tablespoons sesame seeds
4 eggs, omega-3
1 tablespoon ground cinnamon
2 teaspoons mixed spices
1/4 teaspoon nutmeg
2 tablespoons olive oil
1 teaspoon sesame oil
1/2 cup orange flower water
2 cups almond flour (about 7 ounces)
zest of 1 orange, finely grated
zest of 1 lemon, finely grated
5 tablespoons diabetic orange marmalade, more or less to taste
olive oil spray

1. Dry-roast the aniseeds and sesame seeds briefly in a small frying pan. Set aside.
2. Meanwhile beat the eggs with an electric hand-mixer in a medium-size mixing bowl. Mix in the cinnamon, mixed spices, nutmeg, olive oil, sesame oil and the orange flower water.
3. Blend in the almond flour and mix all together to a smooth consistency. Stir in the orange and lemon peel.
4. Sweeten with the orange marmalade to taste. Fold the aniseeds and sesame seeds into the mixture.
5. Spray a square baking dish (8x8 inches) with the olive oil and fill with the cake mixture.
6. Bake in a hot oven 340°F (170°C) for 35-40 minutes, or until golden brown. Check the center for doneness.
7. Allow the cake to cool down. De-mold and cut into equal squares.

Desserts
Apricot Tart
Yield: up to 10 servings

Try the recipe with other fruits. For example peaches or nectarines.

about 1 1/4 pounds ripe apricots
1 'Sweet Paleo Crust' (see page 58), pre-baked
2 teaspoons almond flour
3-4 tablespoons diabetic apricot jam, to taste

1. Wash and dry the apricots. Cut in halves and stone them. Set aside.
2. Sprinkle the pre-baked crust with the almond flour, in order to soak up the fruit juice during the cooking process.
3. Layer the apricots, cut-side up, in concentric circles on top of the crust in the baking dish.
4. Warm up the apricot jam and brush it over the apricots.
5. Bake in a hot oven at 340°F (170°C) for about 35 minutes, or until the dough is golden brown and the apricots are cooked.
6. When you take the tart out of the oven, there might be a film of liquid left on the surface, which will glaze when cooling off.

Desserts
Banana Ice Cream
Yield: about 12 servings (depending on how you scoop it)

In warm weather, this dessert is a favorite with everyone.
Ripe bananas are glycemic, but what the heck – it's still a fairly safe summer treat!
Try serving with raspberry coulis (see recipe page 193).
See also Strawberry Ice Cream (page 202), as well as the Coconut and Chocolate Ice Cream (page 172).

14-ounce can coconut milk
2 tablespoons xylitol, or more to taste
1 tablespoon vanilla extract
1/2 teaspoon xanthan gum
2 eggs, omega-3
4 medium ripe bananas
2 teaspoons fresh lemon juice

1. Combine the coconut milk, xylitol, vanilla extract, xanthan gum and eggs in your blender and mix well.
2. Meanwhile mash the bananas with a fork, together with the lemon juice, and add to the blender. Mix all together.
3. Place the mixture in an ice cream maker and proceed following the instructions of the machine.

If you don't have an ice cream maker then just place the mixture in a bowl, which you then place in the freezer. In this case you need, from time to time, to fold the frozen edges in towards the middle and so entrain air bubbles to lighten the mixture. Do this after 1 hour, once more after the second hour, and then every 30 minutes for the next 2 hours.

Desserts
Banana Pancake
Yield: up to 8 servings

This makes a sweet pancake-style dessert. The use of ripe banana and raisins does mean that it has quite a high sugar content (there is no need for an additional sweetener). For this reason, just treat the dish as a sweetmeat and eat sparingly.

4 tablespoons raisins
1 tablespoon dark rum
1 ripe banana
1 teaspoon lemon juice
3 eggs, omega-3
1 teaspoon ground cinnamon
1 teaspoon vanilla extract
1 tablespoon olive oil
2 tablespoons almond flour
2 tablespoons chopped almonds (or walnuts)
olive oil spray

1. In a small bowl soak the raisins in hot water for about 10 minutes. Drain the raisins, add the rum and mix well. Set aside.
2. Meanwhile mash the banana with a fork and mix in the lemon juice. Set aside.
3. In a medium-size mixing bowl beat the eggs with an electric hand-mixer. Mix in the cinnamon, vanilla extract, olive oil and almond flour and beat all together. Blend in the mashed banana and chopped almonds (or walnuts).
4. Spray a round and flat baking dish (about 10-inch diameter) with the olive oil and spread out the mixture into a thin layer, so it looks like a pancake.
5. Spread out the raisins evenly over the surface of the dish and press in with a fork.
6. Bake in a hot oven at 340°F (170°C) for about 15 minutes, or until the center of the pancake is cooked.

Desserts
Banana-Peach Coconut Flour Gateau
Yield: up to 10 servings

Both the peaches and the bananas are a little glycemic, so not totally conforming. But the pastry is safe and it makes a delicious gateau that will delight your guests – and you are only going to eat one slice!

2 medium-ripe bananas
1 teaspoon of lemon juice
3 eggs, omega-3
2 teaspoons vanilla extract
3 tablespoons olive oil
1/4 cup coconut flour (about 1 ounce)
1/2 teaspoon baking powder
olive oil spray
1 big peach, cut into slices

1. With a fork mash the banana and mix in the lemon juice. Set aside.
2. In a medium-size mixing bowl beat the eggs, vanilla extract and oil with an electric hand-mixer.
3. Mix in the coconut flour and baking powder and blend until the flour is well integrated, which may take a bit longer than with almond flour.
4. Blend in the mashed banana.
5. Spray a round baking mold (approximately 8-9-inch diameter) with the olive oil. Lay out the peach slices in concentric circles on the bottom, keeping the edge of the mold free.
6. Lay out the dough mixture on top of the peaches.
7. Bake in a hot oven at 340°F (170°C) for about 25 minutes, or until the center of the gateau is cooked . Check for doneness.
8. Allow the gateau to cool down. De-mold by putting a serving plate on top and turning the whole lot over. Then lift off the mold, so that the nicely formed underside with the peaches is on top.

Desserts
Blueberry Muffins
Yield: 10 muffins

We found the blueberry muffins are the great standby for the complimentary breakfast in typical American motels. Now you can delight in a fully conforming one in the privacy of your home!

4 eggs, omega-3
1/4 cup light coconut milk
1 1/2 cups almond flour (about 6 ounces)
1/4 cup chia seed flour (about 1 ounce), or flax seed flour
1 teaspoon baking powder
3 tablespoons xylitol, or to taste
2 tablespoons olive oil
1 tablespoon vanilla extract
5 tablespoons fresh blueberries
olive oil spray

1. In a medium-size mixing bowl beat the eggs with an electric hand-mixer. Mix in the coconut milk, the almond flour, the chia seed flour and baking powder. Blend to obtain a smooth consistency.
2. Sweeten with xylitol to taste and mix in the olive oil and vanilla extract.
3. Fold the blueberries into the muffin mixture, using a fork.
4. Spray 10 muffin molds (2.5-inch diameter) with the olive oil and fill with the mixture (3/4 full).
5. Bake in a hot oven at 320°F (160°C) for around 35 minutes, or until the muffins have a golden brown color. Check for doneness.

Desserts
Bond Power Bar
Yield: up to 16 squares

This makes a dense, highly nutritious bar which can be eaten as a snack or for breakfast. It is calorie-dense and the dried apricots are borderline, so don't be tempted to overdo it! (e.g. ration yourself to 1 square per person).

1 cup (16-18 pieces) dried apricots
2 cups walnut pieces (about 8 ounces)
2 eggs, omega-3
1 tablespoon vanilla extract
1/2 of a 3.5-ounce bar dark chocolate of minimum 75% cocoa solids, broken into chips
olive oil spray

1. In a food processor, using the blade, mix the apricots and walnuts until the texture presents a coarse consistency.
2. Blend in the eggs and vanilla extract.
3. Add the chocolate chips at the end and mix briefly, using the 'pulse' button. The chocolate should still present a coarse consistency.
4. Spray an 8x8-inch baking dish with the oil and fill with the mixture.
5. Bake in a hot oven at 340°F (170°C) for about 20 minutes. Check the center for doneness.
6. Allow the dish to cool down. De-mold by flipping it over onto a cutting board. Slice into 16 equal squares.

Desserts
Carrot Cake
Yield: up to 14 servings

At special times of the year we can let things go a little.
The carrot is a bit glycemic – but who's counting?
But when all is said and done, this cake follows the fundamentals: no flour, no butter, no sugar – that's pretty good, and it looks good too – enjoy!

1 cup raisins (about 4.5 ounces)
3 tablespoons dark rum
1 cup walnuts (about 4 ounces), chopped coarsely
5 large eggs, omega-3
4 tablespoons xylitol, or to taste
4 tablespoons almond (or coconut) milk – more if needed for consistency
4 tablespoons olive oil
3 cups almond flour (about 10.5 ounces)
1 teaspoon baking powder
1 teaspoon nutmeg
1 tablespoon ground cinnamon
3 cups grated carrot (about 12 ounces)
olive oil spray
Frosting: around 5.5 ounces of dark chocolate of minimum 75% cocoa solids – approximately 1 1/2 regular (3.5-ounce) bar
4 tablespoons almond (or coconut) milk

1. In a small bowl soak the raisins in hot water for about 10 minutes. Drain the raisins, add the rum and stir in the chopped walnuts. Set aside.
2. Beat the eggs in a large mixing bowl with an electric hand-mixer. Mix in the xylitol, the almond milk and oil, as well as the almond flour, baking powder, nutmeg and cinnamon.
3. Fold in the raisins and walnuts with the rum, as well as the grated carrot.
4. Spray 2 round baking molds (about 8-9-inch diameter each) with the olive oil. Divide mixture into the 2 molds.
5. Bake in a hot oven at 340°F (170°C) for about 25-30 minutes, or until the center of both cakes is cooked. Allow to cool, then de-mold.

Desserts

6. **Frosting:** Meanwhile break the chocolate into small pieces and put into a microwave-proof bowl. Stir in the almond (or coconut) milk.

7. Melt the mixture at half power (about 300 watts) in a microwave oven for approximately 3 minutes. Check and stir every minute. The chocolate should be melted, but avoid overheating.

8. Use as sandwich filling between the two cakes, and as a frosting for the top.

Desserts
Carrot Muffins
Yield: 12 muffins

All the flavors, textures and goodness of carrot cake in a muffin. They are great for continental breakfast – and the kids love them!

3 eggs, omega-3
1 1/2 cups almond flour (about 6 ounces)
1/2 teaspoon baking powder
2 teaspoons ground cinnamon
2 tablespoons olive oil
2 1/2 tablespoons xylitol, or to taste
1 1/2 cup grated carrots (about 6 ounces)
1/2 cup chopped walnuts (about 2 ounces)
olive oil spray

1. In a medium-size mixing bowl beat the eggs with an electric hand-mixer. Mix in the almond flour, baking powder, cinnamon, olive oil and xylitol to taste. Blend to obtain a smooth consistency.
2. Fold in the grated carrots and chopped walnuts.
3. Spray 12 muffin molds (2.5-inch diameter) with the olive oil and fill with the mixture (3/4 full).
4. Bake in a hot oven at 340°F (170°C) for around 20 minutes, or until the center of the muffins is cooked.

Desserts
Chocolate Brownies
Yield: 6 muffins (2.5-inch diameter)

Remarkably, this confection steers its way through a variety of potential pitfalls to provide a brownie that is quite delicious and harmless.

Because the dish is energy dense, it should be eaten in controlled quantities.

2 bars dark chocolate (3.5 ounces **each** – minimum of 75% cocoa solids)
3/4 cup almond (or coconut) milk
1 tablespoon dark rum
4 eggs, omega-3
1 tablespoon xylitol, or to taste
1 teaspoon vanilla extract
optional for Christmas: 1/2 teaspoon allspice
2 tablespoons almond flour
olive oil spray
1 tablespoon almond flakes

1. Break the chocolate into small pieces and put into a medium-size microwave-proof bowl. Add the almond milk.
2. Melt the mixture at half power (about 300 watts) in a microwave oven for approximately 3-4 minutes. Check and stir every minute. The chocolate should be melted, but avoid overheating. Mix in the rum.
3. In a medium-size mixing bowl beat the eggs with an electric hand-mixer. Blend in the xylitol, vanilla extract, allspice (optional for Christmas) and the almond flour.
4. Add the egg mixture to the chocolate mixture and blend to a smooth consistency.
5. Spray 6 muffin molds (2.5-inch diameter) with the olive oil and fill with the mixture. Sprinkle the almond flakes over the surface.
6. Bake in a hot oven at 320°F (160°C) for about 18-20 minutes. The center should still be moist. Check for doneness.

Desserts
Chocolate Cookies
Yield: about 20 cookies (depending on size)

This makes a delicious, chocolate covered cookie with a moist consistency. It is a conforming sweetmeat of the high protein type and should be consumed in limited quantities. Try to eat no more than two at a sitting! Good to eat as a light dessert or with a cup of coffee or tea.
To give a typical Christmas flavor you can add allspice to the chocolate coating.

4 egg whites, omega-3
3 tablespoons xylitol, or to taste
optional for Christmas: 1 tablespoon allspice, or to taste
2 1/4 cups almond flour (about 8 ounces) - add up to 1/4 cup more to achieve a dough-like consistency
1/2 cup chopped almonds (about 2.5 ounces)
Coating:
1/2 of a 3.5-ounce bar dark chocolate of minimum 75% cocoa solids
1 teaspoon orange extract
3 tablespoons fresh orange juice
1 tablespoon rum, dark and flavorful
Garnish:
1 1/2 tablespoons unsweetened shredded coconut
1 tablespoon xylitol
alternatively: 3 tablespoons chopped almond (or hazelnuts)

1. Beat the egg whites in a medium-size mixing bowl with an electric hand-mixer to a stiff consistency.
2. Sweeten with xylitol to taste and (optional for Christmas) the allspice.
3. Mix in carefully the almond flour to obtain a smooth paste. Fold in the chopped almonds.
4. Line a baking tray with non-stick baking paper. Spoon heaped tablespoons of dough onto the baking paper. Press down, flatten and shape into cookies, using a spatula and your fingers.
5. Bake in a hot oven at 340°F (170°C), for about 12 minutes. Check for doneness. Allow the cookies to cool down.
6. **Coating:** break the chocolate into small pieces and put into a small microwave-proof bowl. Add the orange extract and orange

Desserts

juice and melt the mixture in the microwave oven at half power (about 300 watts) for approximately 1 1/2 minutes, stirring once halfway through, until the chocolate is melted. Mix in the rum.

7. Coat the upper-half of the cookies with the chocolate mixture.

8. **Garnish:** Mix the shredded coconut with the xylitol in a little bowl and sprinkle over the chocolate cookies.

(Alternatively, instead of the coconut garnish: sprinkle each chocolate covered cookie with approximately 1/2 teaspoon of chopped almonds and press them into the chocolate with a spatula).

9. Allow the cookies to cool (the chocolate coating has to be solid again). They are now ready for consumption. Store them in a sealed container in your fridge.

Desserts
Chocolate Delight
Yield: up to 10 servings

This recipe provides an impressive and delicious chocolate torte. Because the dish is fundamentally energy dense, you should limit yourself to just one serving at a sitting.
Try serving with raspberry coulis (see recipe page 193).

2 bars dark chocolate (3.5 ounces **each** – minimum of 75% cocoa solids)
3/4 cup almond milk
1 tablespoon dark rum
4 eggs, omega-3
2 tablespoons olive oil
1 teaspoon orange extract
3 tablespoons diabetic orange marmalade
3 tablespoons almond flour
olive oil spray

1. Break the chocolate into small pieces and put into a medium-size microwave-proof bowl. Add the almond milk.
2. Melt the mixture at half power (about 300 Watt) in a microwave oven for approximately 3-4 minutes. Check and stir every minute. The chocolate should be melted, but avoid overheating. Mix in the rum.
3. Meanwhile beat the eggs in a medium-size mixing bowl with an electric hand-mixer. Blend in the olive oil, orange extract, orange marmalade and almond flour.
4. Add the chocolate mixture to the eggs and blend to a smooth consistency.
5. Spray a round, table-ready (say 10-inch diameter) baking dish with the olive oil. Slowly pour the mixture into it.
6. Bake in a hot oven at 340°F (170°C) for about 15 minutes. The center of this chocolate delight should still be slightly moist.
7. Allow to cool before serving.

Desserts
Chocolate Mousse
Yield: 6 servings

This dish is an interesting example of how a superb dessert can be made from high density chocolate and xylitol.
The dish is energy dense – eat sparingly in controlled quantities.

2 bars dark chocolate (3.5 ounces **each** – minimum of 75% cocoa solids)
2 teaspoons orange extract
2 teaspoons instant coffee
4 tablespoons water
4 tablespoons flavorful rum
4 eggs, omega-3, free range
1 1/2 tablespoons xylitol, or to taste (can be replaced by diabetic orange marmalade)
2 teaspoons grated orange peel

1. Break the chocolate into small pieces and put into a medium-size microwave-proof bowl. Add the orange extract, the instant coffee and the water.
2. Melt the mixture at half power (about 300 Watt) in a microwave oven for approximately 3-4 minutes. Check and stir every minute. The chocolate should be melted, but avoid overheating. Mix in the rum and set aside.
3. Meanwhile break the eggs and carefully separate the yolks from the whites into 2 separate mixing bowls.
4. In the first bowl, mix the egg yolks with the xylitol (or orange marmalade) to a creamy texture with an electric hand-mixer. Add 1 teaspoon orange peel and set aside.
5. In the second bowl, beat the egg whites and a pinch of salt with an electric hand-mixer, until very stiff (you can also choose to do it in your food processor).
6. Add the yolk mixture slowly to the cooled down, but still warm, chocolate mixture. Blend to a smooth consistency.
7. Add the egg whites progressively to the mixture, stirring carefully to obtain a smooth, but fluffy chocolate mixture.
8. Spoon the mousse into 6 (depending on size) individual dessert cups. Sprinkle the remaining orange peel over the top.
9. Keep in your fridge (best made the day before consumption).

Desserts
Chocolate Petit Fours
Yield: about 25 servings

This makes a chocolate sweetmeat akin to a chocolate truffle. Treat this as you would a candy and do not overindulge.

Equipment: 25-30 small paper cups (about 1 1/4-inch diameter)

25-30 raisins
3 1/2 tablespoons dark rum
1 orange, preferably organic
3.5-ounce bar dark chocolate (minimum of 75% cocoa solids)
2 teaspoons orange extract
Garnish:
1 tablespoon unsweetened shredded coconut
2 teaspoons xylitol, or to taste

1. In a small bowl soak the raisins in hot water for about 10 minutes. Drain the raisins, add 1/2 tablespoon of rum and mix well. Set aside.
2. Grate the orange skin and set aside the peel. Squeeze the orange and set aside the juice.
3. Break the chocolate into small pieces and put into a small microwave-proof bowl. Add 4 tablespoons of the orange juice and the orange extract. Melt the mixture at half power (about 300 watts) in a microwave oven for approximately 2 minutes. Check and stir twice. The chocolate should be melted, but avoid overheating.
4. Mix the remaining 3 tablespoons of rum and the orange peel into the chocolate.
5. Spoon the chocolate mixture into the paper cups.
6. Press 1 raisin into the center of each cup, using a little spoon.
7. **Garnish:** mix the shredded coconut with the xylitol in a small bowl. Sprinkle the mixture over the top of the 'Petit Fours'.
8. Allow to cool to the point where the chocolate sets. Serve in the paper cups.

Desserts
Citrus Cake
Yield: up to 12 servings

Thanks to Caroline Grossmith for passing on this recipe. This is my version, fine-tuned after several trial runs. It makes an absolutely delicious cake, one which we make all the time.

1 medium orange, preferably organic
1 lemon, preferably organic
4 eggs, omega-3
3-4 tablespoons xylitol, to taste (depending on sweetness of citrus fruits)
3 tablespoons diabetic orange marmalade
1/2 teaspoon bicarbonate of soda
1 tablespoon ground cinnamon
1 tablespoon vanilla extract
1 tablespoon olive oil
1 teaspoon freshly grated ginger
2 cups almond flour (about 7 ounces)
(or: 1 cup almond flour, 1 cup shredded coconut)
2 tablespoons coconut flour
olive oil spray

1. Boil the orange and lemon (whole, unpeeled) for about 10 minutes in a saucepan, until soft. Set aside and let cool.
2. Meanwhile in a medium-size mixing bowl beat the eggs with an electric hand-mixer. Sweeten to taste with the xylitol and orange marmalade.
3. Mix in the bicarbonate of soda, the cinnamon, the vanilla extract, the olive oil and the ginger.
4. Blend in the almond flour (or half almond flour, half shredded coconut) and the coconut flour.
5. Quarter the orange and the lemon, keeping the skin, but discard the pips, the pith of the core and all inedible parts. Blend all together in your food processor. Mix into the cake preparation, together with the fruit juices.
6. Spray a loaf mold (say 9 inches long, 5 inches wide and 3 inches high) with olive oil and fill with the mixture.
7. Bake in a hot oven at 340°F (170°C) for approximately 45-50 minutes, depending on the moistness of the preparation (which mainly depends on the juiciness of the fruits). Check the center of the cake for doneness.

Desserts
Cocoa Muffins
Yield: 7 muffins

This muffin recipe is similar to the Chocolate Brownie recipe (see page 163).
But here we use pure cocoa powder instead of the sweetened chocolate bars, and we sweeten entirely with the safe sugar substitute, xylitol.

1/2 cup unsweetened cocoa powder (about 1.25 ounces)
1/2 teaspoon baking powder
1/2 cup coconut milk
4 eggs, omega-3
3 tablespoons olive oil
1 tablespoon vanilla extract
3/4 cup almond flour (about 3 ounces)
6 tablespoons xylitol, or to taste
olive oil spray
1 tablespoon almond flakes

1. Combine the cocoa powder with the baking powder in a medium-size mixing bowl and pour the coconut milk slowly on top. Mix with an electric hand-mixer.
2. Blend in the eggs, olive oil and vanilla extract.
3. Add the almond flour and blend to a smooth consistency.
4. Sweeten with xylitol to taste.
5. Spray 7 muffin molds (2.5-inch diameter) with the olive oil and fill with the mixture (3/4 full). Sprinkle the almond flakes over the top of muffins.
6. Bake in hot oven at 320°F (160°C) for around 35 minutes. Check the center for doneness.

Desserts
Coconut and Chocolate Gateau
Yield: up to 12 servings

A surprisingly sumptuous and succulent gateau, covered in a chocolate coating, which is quite easy to realize. Taste and enjoy!

4 eggs, omega-3
1 tablespoon vanilla extract
1 tablespoon olive oil
4 tablespoons diabetic orange marmalade, to taste
(can be replaced by 3 1/2 tablespoons xylitol, to taste)
2 cups unsweetened shredded coconut (about 6 ounces)*
1 1/2 cups coconut milk
olive oil spray
Coating: 2/3 of a 3.5-ounce bar dark chocolate of minimum 75% cocoa solids
2 tablespoons dark rum (or 2 tablespoons coconut milk)

1. In a large mixing bowl beat the eggs, vanilla extract, olive oil and the orange marmalade (or xylitol) with an electric hand-mixer.
2. Add the shredded coconut and the coconut milk. Blend well together.
3. Spray a round baking dish (approximately 8-9-inch diameter) with the olive oil and spread out the mixture.
4. Bake in a hot oven at 340°F (170°C) for about 30 minutes. Check for doneness. Allow the gateau to cool down.
5. **Coating:** Meanwhile break the chocolate into small pieces and put into a small microwave-proof bowl. Stir in the rum (or coconut milk).
6. Melt the mixture at half power (about 300 watts) in a microwave oven for approximately 2 minutes. Check and stir twice. The chocolate should be melted, but avoid overheating.
7. With a spatula coat the top of the coconut gateau with the chocolate. Allow to cool before serving.

* The volume compared to weight can vary considerably from one brand to another. Feel free to experiment to discover what works best for you.

Desserts
Coconut and Chocolate Ice Cream
Yield: about 12 servings (depending on how you scoop it)

See also Banana Ice Cream (page 155), as well as the Strawberry Ice Cream (page 202). They are all very popular summer treats. And not to forget – they are made without dairy or bad sugars – so enjoy!
Try serving with raspberry coulis (see recipe page 193).

14-ounce can coconut milk
2 tablespoons xylitol, or more to taste
1 tablespoon vanilla extract
1/2 teaspoon xanthan gum
2 eggs, omega-3
1/2 of a 3.5-ounce bar dark chocolate of minimum 75% cocoa solids, grated

1. Place the coconut milk, the xylitol, the vanilla extract, the xanthan gum and eggs in your blender and mix well.
2. Mix in the chocolate gratings.
3. Place the mixture in an ice cream maker and proceed following the instructions of the machine.

If you don't have an ice cream maker then just place the mixture in a bowl, which you then place in the freezer. In this case you need, from time to time, to fold the frozen edges in towards the middle and so entrain air bubbles to lighten the mixture. Do this after 1 hour, once more after the second hour, and then every 30 minutes for the next 2 hours.

Desserts
Coconut Florentines
Yield: around 12 Florentines (2-inch diameter)

These luxurious, sweet and chewy cookies are ideal to serve when people unexpectedly drop by, or to give as a valued present at Christmas.

3 tablespoons raisins
1 tablespoons dark rum
2 eggs, omega-3
4 tablespoons coconut milk, more or less depending on desired consistency
1 tablespoon olive oil
1 tablespoon vanilla extract
2 teaspoons ground cinnamon, or to taste
1 1/2 cup unsweetened shredded coconut (about 4.5 ounces)*
1 1/2 tablespoons xylitol, or to taste
optional: 6 tablespoons (fully-heaped) coconut flakes

1. In a small bowl soak the raisins in hot water for about 10 minutes. Drain the raisins, add the rum and mix well. Set aside.
2. Break the eggs and carefully separate the yolks from the whites into 2 separate mixing bowls.
3. Add the coconut milk, olive oil, vanilla extract and cinnamon to the egg yolks and blend together with an electric hand-mixer. Mix in the shredded coconut and sweeten with xylitol to taste.
4. Beat the egg whites with an electric hand-mixer, until very stiff.
5. Carefully fold the egg whites into the egg yolk mixture.
6. Optional: fold 4 tablespoons of coconut flakes into the mixture.
7. Using a spoon and your hands, spoon little round heaps, approximately 2-inch diameter, onto a non-stick baking paper. Decorate the top with the remaining coconut flakes (optional).
8. Bake in a hot oven at 320°F (160°C) for about 25 minutes, or until the Florentines have a golden brown color.

*The volume compared to weight can vary considerably from one brand to another. Feel free to experiment to discover what works best for you.

Desserts
Coconut Muffins
Yield: 10 muffins

These muffins are delicious for continental breakfast, at tea-time or as an occasional snack.

4 tablespoons raisins
2 tablespoons dark rum
3 eggs, omega-3
3/4 cup coconut milk
3/4 cup almond flour (about 3 ounces)
1/2 teaspoon baking powder
2 teaspoons ground cinnamon, or to taste
1 tablespoon vanilla extract
1 tablespoon olive oil
1 cup unsweetened shredded coconut (about 3 ounces)*
3 tablespoons diabetic orange marmalade, or to taste
olive oil spray
optional: 1/4 of a 3.5-ounce bar dark chocolate of minimum 75% cocoa solids, broken into small chips

1. In a small bowl soak the raisins in hot water for about 10 minutes. Drain the raisins, add the rum and mix well. Set aside.
2. In a medium-size mixing bowl beat the eggs with an electric hand-mixer. Mix in the coconut milk, almond flour, baking powder, cinnamon, vanilla extract, olive oil and shredded coconut. Blend to a smooth consistency.
3. Blend in the orange marmalade to taste, bearing in mind that you will add other sweetening ingredients (the raisins and the chocolate).
4. Spray 10 muffin molds (2.5-inch diameter) with the olive oil and fill with the mixture.
5. With a fork press raisins and (optional) chocolate chips into each muffin, distributing them equally.
6. Bake in a hot oven at 340°F (170°C) for about 35 minutes, or until the muffins have a golden brown color. Check for doneness.

*The volume compared to weight can vary considerably from one brand to another. Feel free to experiment to discover what works best for you.

Desserts
Coconut Pancake
Yield: up to 8 servings

This makes an aromatic and flavorful, sweetish, yet safe dessert. There is no need for an additional sweetener. It is quite filling and is best thought of as eaten by the slice.

4 tablespoons raisins
1 tablespoon dark rum
1 ripe banana
1 teaspoon lemon juice
3 eggs, omega-3
1 tablespoon vanilla extract
1 tablespoon olive oil
4 tablespoons coconut milk
1 1/2 tablespoons coconut flour
5 tablespoons unsweetened shredded coconut
olive oil spray

1. In a small bowl soak the raisins in hot water for about 10 minutes. Drain the raisins, add the rum and mix well. Set aside.
2. Meanwhile mash the banana with a fork and mix in the lemon juice. Set aside.
3. In a medium-size mixing bowl beat the eggs with an electric hand-mixer. Add the vanilla extract and olive oil. Mix in the coconut milk, coconut flour and shredded coconut. Add the mashed banana.
4. Spray a round and flat baking dish (about 10-inch diameter) with the olive oil and spread out the mixture into a thin layer, so it looks like a pancake.
5. Spread out the raisins evenly over the surface of the dish and press in with a fork.
6. Bake in a hot oven at 340°F (170°C) for about 15 minutes, or until the center of the pancake is cooked.

Desserts
Deviled Strawberries
Yield: 4 servings

This is a fresh, tingling way to spice up strawberries. Strawberries (together with raspberries) are one of the few fruits that are fine eaten at the end of a meal.

1 pound fresh strawberries
1 tablespoon xylitol, or to taste
freshly ground black pepper, to taste
1 tablespoon raspberry vinegar
Garnish: about 30 fresh mint leaves

1. Wash and dry the strawberries. Remove stalks. Cut any big strawberries in half.
2. Place all the strawberries in a medium-size bowl. Sprinkle with the xylitol and pepper generously to taste. Pour the vinegar equally over the berries. Toss very carefully.
3. Best made prior to serving, but allow to chill for 10 minutes.
4. Serve on individual dessert plates and garnish each plate with a few scattered mint leaves.

Desserts
Easy Apple Pie
Yield: up to 12 servings

Try the recipe with other fruits (apricots, nectarines, plums....).

4 tablespoons raisins
1 tablespoon dark rum
olive oil spray
2 medium-size apples (about 14 ounces), unpeeled and sliced
1 1/2 tablespoons xylitol, more or less to taste
Dough:
5 eggs, omega-3
2 tablespoons olive oil
5 tablespoons unsweetened shredded coconut
2 tablespoons xylitol, or to taste
1/2 teaspoon baking powder
2 teaspoons ground cinnamon
1 cup almond flour (about 3.5 ounces)

1. In a small bowl soak the raisins in hot water for about 10 minutes. Drain the raisins, add the rum and mix well. Set aside.
2. Spray a medium-size frying pan with the olive oil and sauté the apples, until they are tender, but not mushy. Stir in the raisins and sweeten with xylitol to taste.
3. Meanwhile, to prepare the dough, beat the eggs with an electric hand-mixer in a medium-size mixing bowl. Add all the dough ingredients and blend to obtain a smooth, albeit quite liquid mixture.
4. Spray a round pie dish (about 8-inch diameter) with the olive oil and spread out a small part of the dough mixture in a thin layer (just to cover the bottom of the dish).
5. Bake in a hot oven at 340°F (170°C) for about 7 minutes, to set the dough. Allow to cool for a few minutes.
6. Lay out apples slices in concentric circles on top of the dough. Flatten the fruit with a fork, but keep edges of crust free.
7. Spread the remaining dough mixture equally over the apples.
8. Return the pie to the hot oven and bake at 340°F (170°C) for about 25 minutes. Check for doneness.
9. Allow the pie to cool down. De-mold by putting a serving plate on top of pie and turning the whole lot over. Then lift off the mold, so that the nicely formed underside of the pie is on top.

Desserts
Jam Crumble Tart
Yield: up to 12 servings

We consider this one of our most scrumptious desserts.
Rather like a treacle tart, without the sin!

Dough:
2 cups almond flour (about 7-8 ounces)
2 tablespoons olive oil
1 tablespoon vanilla extract
1 tablespoon water
2 teaspoons xylitol
1 egg, omega-3

olive oil spray
filling: 8 tablespoons diabetic raspberry jam, or to taste

Crumble:
1/4 cup almond flour (about 1 ounce)
4 tablespoons olive oil
2 tablespoons xylitol, or to taste
1/2 cup unsweetened shredded coconut (about 1.5 ounces)
1 cup chopped walnuts (about 4 ounces)

1. Mix all the dough ingredients in a food processor, using the blade. The dough should form a ball.
2. Spray a 7x9-inch Pyrex dish with olive oil and press the dough into the dish, leaving a 1/2-inch rim around the edges. Prick the bottom of the dough with a fork.
3. Bake in hot oven at 340°F (170°C) for about 10 minutes. Set aside to cool for 5 minutes.
4. Spread the raspberry jam evenly over the warm dough crust.
5. To prepare the crumble, mix the almond flour with the olive oil and xylitol to taste in the food processor.
6. Add the shredded coconut and chopped walnuts and pulse briefly. The crumble should be left coarse and not pulverized.
7. Sprinkle the crumble topping over the raspberry jam.
8. Bake at 340°F (170°C) for another 15-20 minutes, or until the topping is golden brown.
9. Prior to serving, refrigerate for 2-3 hours. Cut into squares.

Desserts
Jeanne's Jam Roly-Poly
Yield: up to 8 servings

Jeanne Bouvet, who is an excellent French cook and long time Natural Eater, along with her husband and two children, has created this beautiful and impressive dessert. The recipe is easy and quick to do.

3 large eggs, omega-3
2 1/2 tablespoons xylitol, or to taste
2 tablespoons olive oil
2 teaspoons vanilla extract
3/4 cup almond flour (about 3 ounces)
6 tablespoons diabetic raspberry or strawberry jam, or more if desired
2 tablespoons almond flakes

1. Line a baking tray with non-stick baking paper. Set aside.
2. Break the eggs and carefully separate the yolks from the whites into 2 separate mixing bowls.
3. Add the xylitol, oil and vanilla extract to the egg yolks and mix with an electric hand-mixer. Blend in the almond flour until smooth. Set aside.
4. Beat the egg whites with an electric hand-mixer, until very stiff.
5. Carefully fold the egg whites into the egg yolk mixture which will give it the appearance of an omelet.
6. Spread out the mixture on the baking paper on the tray with a spatula into a rectangle of around 9x11 inches.
7. Bake in a hot oven at 340°F (170°C) for about 10 minutes. Check the middle of the dough for doneness. Take out of the oven and set aside to cool for 5 minutes.
8. Slide the baked dough on the baking paper onto a work surface. Trim the paper if it helps to the maneuvers.
9. Spread 4 tablespoons of raspberry jam evenly over the dough.
10. With the help of the baking paper carefully roll the gateau into a roll.
11. Place a fairly long serving plate over the roll and turn it carefully over. Remove the baking paper.
12. Spread out the remaining jam over the top and sprinkle with the almond flakes.

Desserts
Lemon and Poppy Seed Muffins
Yield: 8 muffins

These fully conforming muffins with their zingy, lemony taste are a favorite with everyone, young or old.

3 eggs, omega-3
1/4 cup coconut milk
3 tablespoons olive oil
1/4 cup coconut flour (about 1 ounce)
3/4 cup almond flour (about 3 ounces)
1/2 teaspoon baking powder
1 teaspoon ground cinnamon
zest of 1 large lemon (preferably organic), finely grated
1/4 cup freshly squeezed lemon juice
4 tablespoons xylitol, or to taste
2 tablespoons poppy seeds
olive oil spray

1. In a medium-size mixing bowl beat the eggs with an electric hand-mixer. Mix in the coconut milk and olive oil.
2. Add the coconut flour, almond flour, baking powder and blend to obtain a smooth paste.
3. Add the cinnamon, lemon peel and lemon juice and mix well. Sweeten with xylitol to taste and blend in the poppy seeds.
4. Spray 8 muffin molds (2.5-inch diameter) with the olive oil and fill with the mixture (3/4 full).
5. Bake in a hot oven at 320°F (160°C) for around 35 minutes, or until the muffins have a golden brown color. Check for doneness.

Desserts
Lemon Meringue Tart
Yield: up to 12 servings

Ever since he was a little boy, 'Lemon Meringue Tart' was my son Frédéric's favorite dessert. So as soon as I learned Geoff's way of eating, this was the first recipe I adapted to conform to his principles.

Enjoy the fluffy meringue, tangy lemon curd and nutty pastry – just like always. And with this recipe you can do so with a clear conscience!

2 eggs, omega-3
2 tablespoons olive oil
zest of 2 large lemons, finely grated
1/2 cup freshly squeezed lemon juice (from 2 large organic lemons)
7 tablespoons xylitol, or to taste
1 'Sweet Paleo Crust' (see page 58), pre-baked
Meringue:
2 egg whites, omega-3
4 tablespoons xylitol, or to taste

1. Prepare the lemon filling in a medium-size mixing bowl: blend the eggs and oil with an electric hand-mixer. Mix in the lemon peel and lemon juice. Sweeten with xylitol to taste.
2. Slowly pour the filling on top of the pre-baked crust in the baking dish.
3. Bake in a hot oven at 300°F (150°C) for about 30 minutes, or until the filling is cooked. Check for doneness.
Meringue:
4. Pre-heat the grill.
5. Meanwhile beat the egg whites in a medium-size mixing bowl, with a pinch of salt and using an electric hand-mixer, to a stiff consistency. Sweeten with xylitol to taste, by folding it carefully into the egg whites.
6. Spread out the meringue mixture, with a spatula, over the top of the lemon tart.
7. Grill for about 2 minutes, supervising closely, and stop immediately when the meringue shows a light golden color.
8. Allow the tart to cool completely before serving.

Desserts
Marble Ring Cake
Yield: up to 16 servings

This makes a wonderful, fully conforming marble cake that will delight children and adults alike.

5 eggs, omega-3
6 tablespoons xylitol, or to taste
4 tablespoons olive oil
1 teaspoon baking powder
2 cups almond flour (about 7-8 ounces)
2 teaspoons vanilla extract
1/2 cup cocoa powder (about 2 ounces)
1 tablespoon dark rum
4 tablespoons almond milk (more – if needed)
olive oil spray

1. In a medium-size mixing bowl beat the eggs with an electric hand-mixer. Blend in 4 tablespoons of xylitol, 3 tablespoons of olive oil and the baking powder. Add the almond flour and blend to obtain a smooth paste.
2. Split this dough into two equal portions into 2 separate mixing bowls.
3. In one portion blend in the vanilla extract. This will be the 'light colored dough'.
4. In the second portion blend in the remaining 2 tablespoons xylitol, the remaining 1 tablespoon olive oil, the cocoa powder, the rum and the almond milk (add more milk, if the 'dough' is too thick). This will be the 'dark colored dough'.
5. Spray a special ring cake mold with the olive oil. Pour light colored and dark colored dough layers randomly into the mold. You can play with the proportions of light and dark layers to make a yet more interesting 'marbling'.
6. Bake in a hot oven at 340°F (170°C) for about 30 minutes.
7. Check for doneness. The center of the cake should not be moist anymore, but firm.
Fluffy Version:
a) To make a fluffier version of the cake, separate the egg yolks from the egg whites into 2 medium-size mixing bowls.

Desserts

b) Beat the egg yolks with 4 tablespoons of xylitol, 3 tablespoons of olive oil, the baking powder and the almond flour (as in point 1 above). Set aside.

c) With an electric hand-mixer beat the egg whites to a stiff consistency.

d) Fold the egg whites carefully into the egg yolk mixture.

e) Split into 2 equal portions and continue as described in point 3 above.

Desserts
Mock Cheese Cake
Yield: up to 10 servings

This conforming cake can be eaten at any time of day – for example at tea time. It makes also a great dessert after dinner. This is a dense dish that is rich in protein, so ration yourself.

3 tablespoons raisins
1 tablespoon dark rum
1 1/2 cup blanched almonds (about 8 ounces)
1/2 cup almond milk
2 eggs, omega-3
4 1/2 tablespoons xylitol, or to taste
3 tablespoons olive oil
1/4 teaspoon allspice
2 teaspoons vanilla extract
1/2 cup freshly squeezed lemon juice
olive oil spray

1. In a small bowl soak the raisins in hot water for about 10 minutes. Drain, add the rum and mix well. Set aside.
2. Place the almonds in your blender and grind into flour.
3. Add the remaining ingredients and blend until you obtain a very creamy texture.
4. Stir in the raisins.
5. Spray a round, table-ready baking dish (about 9-inch diameter) with the olive oil and fill in the mixture. Alternatively you can fill the mixture into individual ramekins.
6. Bake in a hot oven at 340°F (170°C) for about 20 minutes, or until the center of the cake is cooked.
7. Allow the cake to cool down. Serve in the dish.

Desserts
Nutella Bond

Undeniably there is a market for a harmless chocolate spread. Here we offer our own recipe. It uses regular 'safe' ingredients, but they are concentrated calories, so don't go overboard!

1/4 of a 3.5-ounce bar dark chocolate of minimum 75% cocoa solids
1/4 cup almond milk (or hazelnut milk)
1/4 cup almond butter
1 tablespoon vanilla extract
3 tablespoons unsweetened cocoa powder
2 tablespoons xylitol, or to taste

1. Break the chocolate into small pieces and put into a medium-size microwave-proof bowl. Add the almond milk (or hazelnut milk).
2. Melt the mixture at half power (about 300 watts) in a microwave oven for approximately 40 seconds. Check and stir. The chocolate should be melted, but avoid overheating.
3. Add the almond butter and blend with an electric hand mixer until you obtain a smooth paste.
4. Blend in the vanilla extract, the cocoa powder and sweeten with xylitol to taste.
5. Place the Nutella mixture in a glass jar with a lid and store in your fridge.

Sweetness: True Nutella is, in our view, unpleasantly sweet. It is also not good to habituate the taste buds to excessive sweetness.
Quite deliberately this recipe yields a product which is not so sweet.
Consistency: Adjust the quantities of liquid (almond milk or similar) according to the consistency of the nut butter, so as to obtain a final product which is stiff, yet readily spreadable.

Desserts
Pancake-Waffles
Yield: 6 pancakes (of 5-inch diameter)

This recipe produces something which the Americans would recognize as a pancake, but which the English would think of as a waffle. Of course our recipe is safe and avoids all the bad ingredients.

2 eggs, omega-3
6-8 tablespoons almond milk, depending on the thickness you wish to obtain
1 tablespoon vanilla extract
1 1/2 cups (about 6 ounces) almond flour
1/2 teaspoon baking powder
2 tablespoons xylitol, or to taste.
olive oil spray

1. In a medium-size mixing bowl combine the eggs, the almond milk and vanilla extract and mix with an electric hand-mixer.
2. Add the almond flour and baking powder and mix until smooth.
3. Sweeten with xylitol to taste.
4. Set aside for about 20 minutes.*
5. Spray a non-stick frying pan (or special pancake pan) with olive oil and heat on medium power.
6. Ladle pancake batter in a thin layer into the pan. Cook on medium heat only.
7. When the bubbles begin to burst and the edges begin to brown, it is the moment to flip the waffles. The cooking of the other side will take just under a minute.
8. Repeat with the remaining batter. Makes 6 waffles of 5-inch diameter.
9. Serve on a heated serving dish.

* It is important to let your batter stand for about 20 minutes before cooking the pancake-waffles. The baking powder will have time to activate and will thicken the batter.
Your pancake-waffles will have a fluffier outcome which makes them also easier to turn. It is important to cook them on medium heat.

Desserts
Peach Jelly Mousse
Yield 4 servings

I got the idea after doing a peach jelly and thinking that it would be interesting to change the texture to a mousse-like one. The result is this recipe which achieves perfectly my objectives. Since the peaches are cooked, I don't find them a digestive difficulty when eaten after a meal.

1 pound peaches, pitted and chopped
6 tablespoons orange juice
4-5 tablespoons xylitol (depending on sweetness of the fruit)
4 small gelatin sheets*
1/2 cup coconut milk
1 teaspoon lemon
2 teaspoons vanilla extract
1 sprig fresh mint (for decoration)

1. Place chopped peaches with the orange juice in a medium-size sauce pan. Stir in 3 tablespoons xylitol and bring slowly to a boil. Reduce heat and simmer for about 20 minutes or until fruit has broken down into pulp. Let cool for 5 minutes.
2. Meanwhile soak gelatin sheets in a bowl of cold water for 5 to 10 minutes.
3. Put the coconut milk, lemon juice and vanilla extract in a blender. Add the peach pulp. Blend to a purée.
4. Heat 8 tablespoons (1/2 cup) of peach purée in a small saucepan, but do not boil.
5. Meanwhile lift gelatin sheets from the cold water and squeeze gently to remove excess water. Add to the heated peach mixture in the saucepan, stirring until dissolved.
6. Stir the gelatin mixture into the peach purée in the blender and mix together. Sweeten with the remaining xylitol to taste.
7. Divide the mixture equally amongst 4 dessert glasses or ramekins. Top each serving with mint leaves.
8. Cover and refrigerate until set (at least 4 hours), or until the next day.

* For this recipe I used gelatin sheets measuring 4.6 x 2.75 inches. Can be replaced by agar-agar which is a seaweed extract and is used as a vegan thickener. It can be found in every Health Food Store and online.

Desserts
Peach Tart Tatin
Yield: up to 12 servings

The original French recipe is made with apples. You can use any fruit in season.
The peaches, being cooked, there should not be a digestive difficulty serving the tart even at the end of a meal.

olive oil spray
1 pound peaches, sliced
3 eggs, omega-3
2 tablespoons olive oil
1 teaspoon mixed spices
2 teaspoons vanilla extract
1/4 cup coconut milk
4 tablespoons diabetic orange marmalade, or to taste
1 cup almond flour (about 3.5 ounces)
1/2 cup unsweetened shredded coconut (about 1.5 ounces)*

1. Spray a round baking dish (about 8-inch diameter) with the olive oil and lay out the peaches in a double layer in concentric circles on the bottom of the dish.
2. In a medium-size mixing bowl beat the eggs. Mix in the oil, mixed spices, vanilla extract, coconut milk and orange marmalade to taste. Blend in the almond flour and shredded coconut.
3. Cover the peaches in the baking dish with the dough mixture.
4. Bake in a hot oven at 340°F (170°C) for about 30- 35 minutes. Check the center for doneness.
5. Allow the tart to cool down. De-mold by putting a serving plate on top and turning the whole lot over. Then lift off the mold, so that the nicely formed underside with the peaches is on top.

* The volume compared to weight can vary considerably from one brand to another. Feel free to experiment to discover what works best for you.

Desserts
Pecan Nut Cake
Yield: up to 15 servings (slices)

This is our classic cake recipe made special with the seductive flavors and texture of pecan nuts.

5 tablespoons raisins
1 tablespoon dark rum
5 eggs, omega-3
1 cup almond milk (or coconut milk)
1 tablespoon ground cinnamon
1 tablespoon olive oil
2 teaspoons vanilla extract
2 teaspoons ground mixed spices
2 1/4 cups almond flour (about 8 ounces – more or less depending on egg size)
4-6 tablespoons diabetic orange marmalade, to taste
1 cup pecan nut pieces (about 4.5 ounces)
olive oil spray

1. In a small bowl soak the raisins in hot water for about 10 minutes. Drain the raisins, add the rum and mix well. Set aside.
2. In a medium-size mixing bowl beat the eggs with an electric hand-mixer. Mix in the almond milk, cinnamon, olive oil, vanilla extract and mixed spices.
3. Blend in the almond flour and orange marmalade to taste.
4. Stir the pecan nut pieces and the raisins into the dough.
5. Spray an 8x8-inch square loaf mold, or any other similar loaf mold, with the olive oil and fill with the mixture.
6. Bake in a hot oven at 340°F (170°C) for about 35-40 minutes. Check the center for doneness.
7. Allow the cake to cool down. De-mold or serve in the loaf mold.

Desserts
Poppy Seed and Apple Gateau
Yield: up to 12 servings

Geoff's earliest memories are of his Czech grandmother's delicious poppy-seed patisserie (such as koláčky and buchty). Central European cooking uses blue seeds (Asian poppy-seed is white) which have a pleasing, nutty taste. They do have some useful micronutrients but, since poppy seed is only used in condiment quantities, the contribution is modest. Fortunately this goes for the microscopic amounts of opium in them too!

2 small-medium apples (about 3/4 pound)
1/4 cup freshly squeezed lemon juice
2 tablespoons rum
3 tablespoons diabetic orange marmalade
1 teaspoon freshly grated ginger
1 teaspoon ground cinnamon
1 teaspoon vanilla extract
3 tablespoons poppy seeds
4 tablespoons xylitol, or to taste
5 eggs, omega-3
1 tablespoon olive oil
7 tablespoons almond flour (about 1/2 cup)
olive oil spray

1. Grate the apples with the skin and transfer into a medium-size mixing bowl.
2. Mix in the lemon juice, rum, orange marmalade, grated ginger, cinnamon and vanilla extract. Mix in the poppy seeds and sweeten with xylitol to taste. Set aside.
3. Take 2 eggs and carefully separate the yolks from the whites into 2 separate mixing bowls. Set aside the egg whites.
4. Add the remaining 3 eggs to the yolks in the bowl. Beat with an electric hand-mixer and blend in the oil and almond flour.
5. Fold the apple mixture into the egg mixture. Set aside.
6. Meanwhile beat the egg whites with an electric hand-mixer, until very stiff.
7. Carefully fold the egg whites into the apple-egg mixture.
8. Spray a round and flat (about 9 or 10-inch diameter) table-ready baking dish with the olive oil and fill with the mixture.
9. Bake in a hot oven at 340°F (170°C) for about 30 mins. Check the center for doneness. Allow to cool and serve in the dish.

Desserts
Poppy Seed Coconut Bar
Yield: up to 10 bars (3.5-4 inches long)

This is an energy bar variant with its poppy seeds, zingy taste and filling consistency. Great for that occasional snack.

6 eggs, omega-3
1/2 cup coconut flour (about 2 ounces)
1 teaspoon baking powder
1/2 teaspoon xanthan gum
4 tablespoons olive oil
4 tablespoons xylitol, or more to taste
4 tablespoons lemon juice
1 tablespoon grated lemon peel
3 tablespoons poppy seeds
2 teaspoons freshly grated ginger
olive oil spray

1. In a medium-size mixing bowl beat the eggs and the coconut flour with an electric hand-mixer. Blend in the baking powder, xanthan gum, olive oil and sweeten with xylitol to taste.
2. Mix in the lemon juice and lemon peel, as well as the poppy seeds and ginger.
3. Spray a special baking mold (for bars) with olive oil and fill with the mixture (3/4 full).
4. Bake in a hot oven at 340°F (170°C) for about 25-30 minutes. Check the center for doneness.

Desserts
Prune Truffles
Yield: about 16-20 truffles

I just can't stop myself searching out new ways to make succulent treats! These truffles have an incredibly zingy taste and they melt in the mouth. They are energy dense – so do just restrict yourself to a couple at most.

Dried plums (prunes) are a little glycemic, but hey – they do provide dietary fiber, a host of micronutrients, and they even help bone building!

1 cup pitted prunes (about 20 prunes)
3/4 cup grapefruit juice
2/3 of a 3.5-ounce bar dark chocolate (of 75% cocoa solids)
1 tablespoon vanilla extract
1/2 cup unsweetened shredded coconut (about 1.5 ounces)*
optional: 1 tablespoon xylitol, or to taste

1. Cover the prunes with grapefruit juice and soak for 1 hour.
2. Break the chocolate into small pieces into a medium-size microwave-proof bowl and add 3 tablespoons of grapefruit juice (from the prune soaking liquid).
3. Melt the chocolate at half power (about 300 Watt) in a microwave oven for approximately 2 minutes. Check and stir twice. The chocolate should be melted, but avoid overheating. Set aside.
4. Meanwhile place prunes with the juice in a food processor, and using the blade, pulse until smooth.
5. Pulse in vanilla extract and melted chocolate. Proceed until you obtain a smooth mixture.
6. Store the mixture in a bowl in your freezer for about 1 hour.
7. Remove from freezer. Scoop out little amounts of mixture with a small spoon (and use of fingers) to form small 1-inch balls.
8. Mix shredded coconut and xylitol (optional: you may find the truffle already sweet enough) on a plate and coat the truffles, using your fingers.
9. Store truffles flat, without stacking, in a container in your freezer and remove only prior to serving.

* The volume compared to weight can vary considerably from one brand to another.

Desserts
Raspberry Coulis
Yield: about 1½ cups

This coulis serves as an accompaniment to a wide variety of desserts (e.g. chocolate desserts or ice creams). Can be served warm or chilled, depending on the dessert.

This recipe can also be done with other fruits, such as strawberries, blackcurrants, peaches and so forth.

1 packet frozen raspberries (12-16 ounces)
1 teaspoon lemon juice, to taste
5 tablespoons xylitol, more or less to taste

1. Defrost the raspberries in a colander, but collect the juice.
2. Mix the raspberries and juice in a food processor or blender.
3. Rub the purée with a wooden spoon through a sieve, to strain out the seeds. This needs a little time to do.
4. Mix in the lemon juice and sweeten with xylitol to taste.

Desserts
Raspberry Crumble
Yield: up to 6 servings

Unlike a conventional fruit crumble, the fruit here is not stewed. The frozen raspberries already have the right consistency.
The dish makes a delicious dessert to be eating in moderate quantities.

1 packet frozen raspberries (about 12-16 ounces)*
olive oil spray
2 1/2 tablespoons xylitol, to taste
Crumble:
2 egg yolks, omega-3
3 tablespoons olive oil
2 tablespoons xylitol, or to taste
about 1 1/2 cups almond flour (about 6 ounces)

1. Defrost the raspberries and set aside in a colander.
2. Spray a square, table-ready baking dish (8x8 inches) with the olive oil and spread out the fruits (the fruit juice should not exceed 1 tablespoon). Sprinkle xylitol to taste over the top.
Crumble:
3. In a medium-size mixing bowl beat the egg yolks, olive oil and xylitol to taste with a hand-whisk. Mix in the almond flour, and by hand, knead the mixture into a ball.
4. Leave the pastry, without crumbling it, to rest in a cool place, or in your fridge, for at least 1 hour, the time needed for the almond flour to thoroughly absorb the oil. It will now be easy to crumble and to cook. If not, the almond flour will suck up the fruit juice of the raspberries during the cooking process, which will then make it a kind of doughy porridge.
5. Using your hands, crumble the dough over the fruit in the baking dish.
6. Bake in a hot oven at 340°F (170°C) for about 15-20 minutes, or until golden brown. Check for doneness.

* If you replace the red berries by a different fruit, avoid an excess of fruit juice. If needed, pre-cook the fruits for a few minutes, then drain and spread out the fruits in the baking dish. Pour just 1 tablespoon of juice over the fruits and sprinkle with xylitol to taste (see above).

Desserts
Raspberry Sorbet
Yield: 4 servings

A classic sorbet that is safe and healthy to eat. You can also use other berries instead.

1 packet frozen raspberries (12 ounces)
1/4 cup water
4 1/2 tablespoons xylitol, or to taste
2 egg whites, omega-3
2 teaspoons freshly squeezed lemon juice

1. Defrost the raspberries in a colander, but collect the juice.
2. Place the berries with their juice, together with the water and 3 tablespoons of xylitol, in a small saucepan and bring to a boil. Cook on low heat for about 5 minutes. Add the remaining xylitol to taste. Allow to cool.
3. Place the egg whites in a blender (or food processor), add the cooled berries and the lemon juice. Purée all together.
4. Place the mixture in an ice cream maker and proceed following the instructions of the machine.

If you don't have an ice cream maker then just place the mixture in a bowl, which you then place in the freezer. In this case you need, from time to time, to fold the frozen edges in towards the middle and so entrain air bubbles to lighten the mixture. Do this after 1 hour, once more after the second hour, and then every 30 minutes for the next 2 hours.

Desserts
Red Berry Muffins
Yield: 6 muffins

Missing your continental breakfast? Here is a simple solution. These muffins are delicious with a cup of coffee in the morning - or indeed at any time of day.

1 small punnet fresh raspberries or strawberries (about 5.5 ounces)
4 1/2 tablespoons xylitol, or to taste
2 egg whites, omega-3
1/2 cup well packed almond flour (about 2 ounces)
1 teaspoon orange extract
olive oil spray

1. Check the raspberries for cleanliness, wiping as necessary - don't wash. Set aside six raspberries for decoration.
If you use strawberries, wash them carefully and wipe dry. Set aside 3 strawberries, cut in half, for decoration. Cut the remaining strawberries into small pieces.
2. Sprinkle the berries with 2 tablespoons of xylitol. Set aside.
3. With an electric hand-mixer beat the egg whites in a medium-size mixing bowl to a stiff consistency. Fold in carefully the almond flour and orange extract. Sweeten with the remaining xylitol to taste and fold in the berries.
4. Spray 6 muffin molds (2.5-inch diameter) with the olive oil. Divide the mixture equally into each mold.
5. Cook in a hot oven at 340°F (170°C) for about 20 minutes, or until golden brown.
6. Check for doneness. Remove the muffins from the oven and set aside to cool.
7. De-mold the muffins. Decorate each muffin with one raspberry, or 1 strawberry half, and serve either warm or cold.

Desserts
Rich Christmas Cake
Yield: up to 14 servings

Yes, your Christmas can still have its cake–and you can eat it too! This recipe contains all the special Christmassy ingredients, but avoids the pitfalls of bad fats, starches and sugars. Your guests won't know the difference.

1 medium orange, preferably organic
5 tablespoons raisins
1/3 cup chopped dried figs (about 4 figs)
1/3 cup chopped dried apricots (about 5 apricots)
3 tablespoons rum, dark and flavorful
2 cups mixed raw nuts (chopped almonds, chopped walnuts and chopped pecan nuts – about 9 ounces all together)
6 eggs, omega-3
2 tablespoons olive oil
1 tablespoon vanilla extract
2 teaspoons orange extract
1 tablespoon allspice, or to taste
about 2 1/2 cups almond flour (about 9 ounces)
1 1/2 teaspoons baking powder
5-6 tablespoons diabetic orange marmalade, to taste
olive oil spray

1. Grate the orange skin and set aside the peel. Squeeze the orange to obtain about 1/4 cup of juice. Set aside.
2. In a bowl soak the raisins in hot water for 10 minutes. Drain them and combine with the figs and apricots in a medium-size bowl. Mix in the rum and fold in the chopped nuts. Set aside.
3. Meanwhile take a medium-size mixing bowl, and with an electric hand-mixer, beat the eggs with the olive oil, vanilla extract, orange extract and allspice to taste.
4. Mix in the orange juice, orange peel, the almond flour and baking powder. Sweeten with the orange marmalade to taste.
5. Fold in the raisins, figs, apricots and mixed nuts.
6. Spray a cake mold (9 inches long, 5 inches wide and 3 inches high) with olive oil and fill with the cake mixture.
7. Bake in a hot oven at 340°F (170°C) for about 40 minutes, or until golden brown. Check for doneness.
8. Allow to cool down and de-mold.

Desserts
Rocky Road Chocolate Bar
Yield: about 8 servings

This makes a yummy, crunchy chocolate seed and nut bar. The recipe for the 'Three Flour Cracker' (see page 60) is one that has been developed in conjunction with **UGGFoods.com** and, if you find it easier, order the ready-made mix from them.

3.5-ounce bar dark chocolate of minimum 75% cocoa solids
1 tablespoon agave syrup
3 tablespoons raisins
1 tablespoon dark rum
1/2 tablespoon vanilla extract
1 handful (about 1 ounce) raw chopped cashew nuts
1 handful (about 1 ounce) raw chopped walnuts
5-6 'Three Flour Crackers' (see page 60) - about 1 1/2 - 2 ounces

1. Break the chocolate into small pieces and put into a medium-size microwave-proof bowl, together with the agave syrup.
2. Melt the chocolate at half power (about 300 watts) in a microwave oven for about 2 minutes. Check and stir twice. The chocolate should be melted, but avoid overheating.
3. Meanwhile take a small bowl and soak the raisins in hot water for about 10 minutes. Drain the raisins, add the rum and mix well. Set aside.
4. Stir the vanilla extract and the nuts into the melted chocolate.
5. Using your hands, crumble the crackers into small flakes. Stir into the chocolate, so that the flakes are well coated.
6. Stir in the raisins with the rum.
7. Divide the mixture into 2 small special bar-shaped silicon molds (about 4 x 2.5 inches - alternatively use muffin molds). Press into the molds to a depth of about 3/4 inch.
8. Store in your fridge until set. Then de-mold. When finished the product should look like a thick, chunky chocolate bar.

Desserts
Sesame Cookies
Yield: about 15 cookies (2-inch diameter)

These Asian-style cookies aren't overly sweet and have a wonderful crunch from the sesame seeds. The sesame paste 'tahini' (which replaces dairy butter) brings its own delicious texture and flavor.

They're the ideal accompaniment to a freshly brewed cup of coffee or tea.

1 1/4 cups almond flour (about 5 ounces)
1/2 teaspoon baking powder
6 tablespoons water
5 tablespoons ready-made sesame paste, also called 'tahini'
2 tablespoons olive oil
1 tablespoon vanilla extract
2 1/2 tablespoons xylitol, to taste
4 tablespoons sesame seeds
Garnish: 2 tablespoons pumpkin seeds

1. Combine the almond flour and baking powder in a medium-size mixing bowl. Add the water, tahini, olive oil and vanilla extract, and using an electric hand-mixer, blend to obtain a smooth paste.
2. Sweeten with xylitol to taste. Mix the sesame seeds into the dough.
3. Line a baking tray with non-stick baking paper. Spoon heaped tablespoons of dough onto the baking paper. Press down, flatten and shape into cookies, using a spatula and your fingers.
4. Decorate each cookie with a few pumpkin seeds.
5. Bake in a hot oven at 320°F (160°C) for about 30 minutes, or until lightly brown. Check for doneness.
6. Let cool on the baking sheet.
7. Can be stored in a cookie jar in your fridge for some time, since these cookies are made without eggs.

Desserts

Spicy Christmas Cookies

Yield: about 25-30 small cookies

This cookie recipe has all those wondrous spices redolent of Christmas: cloves, aniseed, ginger, nutmeg, rose water and so forth. Enjoy at any time of the year!

2 eggs, omega-3
4-5 tablespoons diabetic orange marmalade, to taste
1 3/4 cup almond flour (about 7 ounces)
4 tablespoons olive oil
2 tablespoons rose water
1 tablespoon ground cinnamon
2 teaspoons nutmeg
1 teaspoon allspice
1/2 teaspoon ground cloves
2 teaspoons ground ginger (or 1 teaspoon freshly grated ginger)
3 tablespoons sesame seeds
optional (depending on taste): 2 tablespoons aniseeds

Coating:
1/2 of a 3.5-ounce bar dark chocolate (75% cocoa solids)
1 teaspoon orange extract
3 tablespoons orange juice
1 tablespoon rum, dark and flavorful

1. In a medium-size mixing bowl beat the eggs and orange marmalade (to taste) with an electric hand-mixer. Blend in the almond flour, olive oil and rose water. Mix in the cinnamon, nutmeg, allspice, cloves and ginger. Stir in the sesame seeds and (optional) the aniseeds. Blend to obtain a "thick dough".

2. Line a baking tray with non-stick baking paper. Spoon heaped tablespoons of dough onto it. Press down, flatten and shape into small cookies, using a spatula and your fingers.

3. Bake in a hot oven at 340°F (170°C) for about 15 minutes. Check for doneness.

4. **Coating:** break the chocolate into small pieces and put into a small microwave-proof bowl. Add the orange extract, orange juice and melt the mixture in the microwave oven at half power (about 300 watts) for approximately 1 1/2 minutes, stirring once halfway through, until the chocolate is melted. Stir in the rum.

5. Coat the upper-half of the cookies with the chocolate mixture. Let them cool.

Desserts
Strawberry and Banana Terrine
Yield: about 6 servings

This is a very colorful and refreshing dish – serve on hot summer days.

1 pound strawberries
10 small gelatin sheets (4.6 x 2.75 inches)
1 1/2 cups grapefruit juice
1 1/2 cups orange juice
3 tablespoons xylitol, or to taste
2 tablespoons fresh mint leaves
1 big ripe banana (about 1/2 pound)

1. Wash and dry the strawberries. Cut in half, separate into 2 lots and set aside.
2. Soak gelatin sheets in a bowl of cold water for 5-10 minutes.
3. Meanwhile combine the two juices together in a small saucepan. Bring to a boil. Sweeten with xylitol to taste. Set aside for 5 minutes to cool.
4. Lift gelatin sheets from the cold water and squeeze gently to remove excess water. Stir into the warm juices until dissolved.
5. Take a transparent Pyrex cake mold (for example 9.5 inches long, 4 inches wide and 3 inches high) and pour 1/2 inch of the jelly juice on the bottom. Lay out a few mint leaves. Allow the jelly to set in the freezer for about 25 minutes.
6. Take the mold out of the freezer and lay out the first lot of strawberries on the jelly. Pour some more jelly juice in between and on top of the fruit. Lay out a few mint leaves. Allow to set in the freezer for about 25 minutes.
7. Meanwhile slice the banana. Take the mold out of the freezer and add the slices in a layer on the jelly. Pour some jelly juice in between and on top. Lay out a few mint leaves. Allow to set in the freezer for about 25 minutes.
8. Take the mold out of the freezer and add the remaining strawberries in a layer. Lay out the remaining mint leaves. Pour the remaining jelly juice on top and allow to set in the freezer for about 25 minutes.
9. Store in your fridge. This desert is best made the day before serving. Serve in the dish.

Desserts
Strawberry Ice Cream
Yield: up to 14 servings (depending on how you scoop it)

When I had finished refining this recipe, it came out more like a sorbet, with little fat or 'cream'. It is absolutely delicious and leaves a clean taste on the palate. Here we do not use eggs either, which makes the dish low fat.

See also Banana Ice Cream (page 155), as well as the Coconut and Chocolate Ice Cream (page 172).

Everybody loves these delicious and safe ice cream recipes, since they are made without dairy and sugar which are the usual bad ingredients in conventional ice creams.

2 pounds frozen strawberries
1 cup rich coconut milk (Thai style)
10 tablespoons diabetic strawberry jam
2 tablespoons vanilla extract
1 teaspoon xanthan gum
4-5 tablespoons xylitol, to taste

1. Defrost the strawberries in a colander a few hours prior to the preparation. Set aside a few berries for decoration.
2. Place strawberries in your food processor and purée until smooth.
3. Mix in the coconut milk, strawberry jam, vanilla extract and xanthan gum. Sweeten with xylitol to taste.
4. Place the mixture in an ice cream maker and proceed following the instructions of the machine.

If you don't have an ice cream maker then just place the mixture in a bowl, which you then place in the freezer. In this case you need, from time to time, to fold the frozen edges in towards the middle and so entrain air bubbles to lighten the mixture. Do this after 1 hour, once more after the second hour, and then every 30 minutes for the next 2 hours.

Desserts
Strawberry Jam Quick-Fix
Yield: about 2 ½ cups

This is a healthful and sugar-free replacement for conventional jam.

The special gelling qualities of chia seed perform the function of pectin in conventional jams.

1 pound strawberries, cleaned and cut in half
6 tablespoons chia seeds
about 9 tablespoons xylitol, more or less to taste
1-2 tablespoons water (only if needed for thickness)

1. Blend the strawberries in your food processor, using the blade.
2. Blend in the chia seeds, xylitol to taste, and if needed for thickness, add some water.
3. Let stand for a 30 minutes, or until the mixture thickens.
4. Xylitol is as good a preservative as sugar, but since we use much less xylitol than conventional jams use sugar, and since it is not cooked, we suggest consuming fairly quickly. Store in a sealed container in the fridge.
5. To eat as a compôte dessert, reduce the quantity of xylitol to taste.

Desserts
Turkish Coconut Delight
Yield: up to 16 servings

The Rock Hotel, Kyrenia, in the culturally Turkish part of Cyprus, served us this delicious sweetmeat.
We asked to see the chef and he very kindly gave us his recipe. I have adapted it to make it conforming to the Bond Precepts.

14-ounce can rich coconut milk
3 tablespoons agar-agar flakes*
3 1/2 tablespoons xylitol, or to taste
1 tablespoon vanilla extract
1 3/4 cup unsweetened shredded coconut (about 5 ounces)**
olive oil spray

1. Empty the coconut milk into a pan and stir in the agar-agar flakes (or powder). Use a hand-whisk to avoid clumping.
2. Bring slowly to a boil, then simmer for about 3 minutes, stirring frequently with the hand whisk and following the instructions on the agar-agar packet.
3. Sweeten with xylitol to taste.
4. Add the vanilla extract and blend in the shredded coconut.
5. Spray an 8x8-inch Pyrex dish with olive oil and spread out the mixture, flattening with a spatula. Set aside to cool.
6. Prior to serving, cut into equal squares (2x2 inches), or cut out rounds with a 2-inch diameter cookie cutter.

* Agar-agar is a seaweed extract and is used as a vegan thickener. It can be found in every Health Food Store and online.
If you use the powder form of agar-agar, reduce the quantity for the above recipe by a third to 1 tablespoon.
** The volume compared to weight can vary considerably from one brand to another. Feel free to experiment to discover what works best for you.

Desserts
Walnut Chocolate Cookies
Yield: about 18-20 cookies (2-inch diameter)

Our basic cookie recipe with the added zing of allspice, chocolate and crunchy walnut pieces.

1 cup almond flour (about 3.5 ounces)
1/2 cup unsweetened shredded coconut (about 1.5 ounces)*
1/2 teaspoon baking powder
1/2 cup almond milk
4 tablespoons olive oil
1 tablespoon vanilla extract
1 teaspoon allspice
4 tablespoons xylitol, or to taste
1/2 cup walnut pieces (about 2 ounces)
1/2 of a 3.5-ounce bar dark chocolate minimum 75% cocoa solids

1. Combine in a medium-size mixing bowl the almond flour, shredded coconut and baking powder.
2. Add the almond milk, olive oil, vanilla extract and allspice. Mix all together with an electric hand-mixer.
3. Sweeten with xylitol to taste.
4. Chop the walnut pieces in your food processor, by pulsing briefly, using the blade. Fold into the dough.
5. Break the chocolate into pieces and place in your food processor. Using the blade, pulse to obtain small chips. Fold into the dough mixture which will have a slightly coarse consistency.
6. Line a baking tray with non-stick baking paper. Spoon heaped tablespoons of dough onto the baking paper. Press down, flatten and shape into cookies of about 2-inch diameter, using a spatula and your fingers.
7. Bake in a hot oven at 320°F (160°C) for about 30 minutes. Check for doneness.
8. Let cool on the baking sheet.
9. Can be stored in a cookie jar in the fridge for some time, since these cookies are made without eggs.

*The volume compared to weight can vary much from one brand to another.

INDEX

INDEX

INDEX

POULTRY, GAME & MEAT

INDEX

SEAFOOD

DESSERTS

INDEX

INDEX

AFTERWORD
From Geoff Bond

I passionately believe in the insights contained in the science of Nutritional Anthropology. My driving motivation is to stimulate everyone, no matter what your origins and background, to improve your lives. I hope that this recipe book has inspired and encouraged you to know more. Your first port of call should be my website: www.TheBondEffect.com. There you will find online support, speaking engagements, breaking news, updates, hints and tips, and much more. In addition, you can acquire access to many other support materials.

Deadly Harvest - The Bond Effect "Bible"
ISBN: 978-0-7570-0142-0

As a Nutritional Anthropologist, I have combined the latest scientific research with insightful studies of primitive tribal lifestyles to understand how to live in a way our body recognizes. With Deadly Harvest in hand, you will come to see how diseases like cancer, heart disease, stroke, diabetes, obesity, arthritis, osteoporosis, allergies, ADHD, autism and Alzheimer's are not inevitable, but are optional. They are due to the mismatch between the lifestyle designed by our evolutionary history, and the lifestyle we live today. Fully explained in plain English, you will understand how modern diets are truly killing us, and what you can do to improve our health, combat illnesses, and live longer. It provides an easy-to-follow blueprint to take back control of your life.

The Bond Briefing
Everyone serious about adopting the Bond Effect will find the monthly Briefing an indispensable aid to keep focused on the essentials. The Bond Briefing takes no advertising – and so it is free to give an honest, straight-from-the-shoulder, Bond Effect viewpoint. More at www.TheBondEffect.com.